Joining the Dots

A Beginner's Guide to Listening to Classical Music

Steve Hobson

Joining the Dots

A Beginner's Guide to Listening to Classical Music

Matador
9 De Montfort Mews
Leicester LE1 7FW, UK
Tel: (+44) 116 255 9311 / 9312
Email: books@troubador.co.uk
Web: www.troubador.co.uk/matador

ISBN 9781-848760-219

British Library Cataloguing in Publication Data.
A catalogue record for this book is available from the British Library.

Typeset in 12pt Bembo by Troubador Publishing Ltd, Leicester, UK
Printed in the UK by TJ International, Padstow, Cornwall

Matador is an imprint of Troubador Publishing Ltd

This book is dedicated to the memory of my father,

Thomas G Hobson (1906 – 1981),

and to my mother,

Clarice E Hobson (1912 – 2007)

I would like to thank my wife, Elisabeth, for her patience in checking the manuscript of this book, and the way she has ensured that I meant what I said and said what I meant.

Caliban:

Be not afeard; the isle is full of noises,
Sounds and sweet airs, that give delight, and hurt not.
Sometimes a thousand twangling instruments
Will hum about mine ears; and sometimes voices,
That, if I then had wak'd after long sleep,
Will make me sleep again: and then, in dreaming,
The clouds methought would open, and show riches
Ready to drop upon me; that, when I wak'd,
I cried to dream again

The Tempest, Act III, Scene 2
William Shakespeare

Contents

Introduction

What is this book about?

This book is about listening to classical music. It talks about how to listen to it, and why you might want to listen to it in the first place.

There is nothing magical about listening to this kind of music, and anyone can enjoy it. There is good classical music, and there is not-so-good classical music, just as there is with everything people do, from building bridges to cooking meals.

Indirectly, I suppose, it is also about me, and how I grew to love this music. I have described this process of learning about music, not to show how incredibly clever or lucky I was, but because it might help you understand why I bothered to listen when there was so much other music around, from The Beatles to Louis Armstrong.

Part One charts the musical knowledge that we all bring with us from the womb, and describes my early encounters with music of all kinds.

Part Two concerns itself with the history of Western music, insofar as it is relevant to the listener. For example, the fact that Mozart wrote his music in the eighteenth century rather than the twentieth century is important, because it affects our expectations and affects what Mozart is trying to communicate to us. The fact that he was born in Salzburg rather than Vienna, however, doesn't affect our listening at all.

This part of the book examines all periods, but concentrates particularly on music of the twentieth century, because listeners often find this music difficult or puzzling, and because it is music that speaks to us of our time.

It's not essential to know about the history to enjoy the music, and it's something you can pick up on the way, when and as you need it. But it's interesting to know a bit about the background of the music you're listening to.

Part Three is a guide to listening to new music – what to expect, what to listen for, and how to make sense of it. Examples from contemporary composers are explained, as well as how to approach the experience of live concerts.

What is this book not about?

This book is not an encyclopaedia of classical music. There are no life stories of the 'great' composers or performers.

It is not a manual for musicians. I am not a musician myself, and it would be wrong of me to write for people who produce the very stuff I'm writing about. Like many people my age, I did learn to play acoustic guitar by ear, and I had a disastrous two weeks at school trying, unsuccessfully, to get a sound out of a flute. Later in life I played the piano, after a fashion, but that was as a result of my love of music, not the cause of it.

The book is not about treating you as a child who wants a diet of sweets. You are an adult, quite capable of appreciating grown-up food. There are no cartoons or flashy graphics. It is a book about music, written for adults.

You don't need any musical knowledge to read and understand this book. You don't need to know the difference between a crotchet and a minim, a sharp and a flat, or Beethoven and Mozart. You just need a certain amount of curiosity and open-mindedness.

I don't deal with opera or with film music, and there are many composers – including some very important ones – that don't get a look-in. This is not a function of quality or value – I just had to draw the line somewhere. It is a function of time and space.

Why should I read it?

- Maybe you have heard some classical music – on the radio, in an advert, in a film, even in a lift – and you would like to know more about it. This book will help.

- Perhaps you already love pop music, or another kind of music, and think classical music is old-fashioned, or boring, and you can't see what the fuss is about. This book will give you even more music to listen to and love.

- Maybe someone has told you, or suggested to you, that classical music is difficult to understand without a special key. This book will show you that the door is already wide open, and you already have the key anyway.

- Maybe you feel that classical music is all about dead men and old audiences. This book will introduce you to contemporary music, by living composers who write about modern issues, like the terrorist attack on the World Trade Centre, or football, or war.

- It's possible you were put off classical music at school. Don't worry – this is not a textbook, and it contains no tests, quizzes, or self-assessment questions!

But the main reason to read this book is to open up a world of experience and beauty that is so powerful that they sent it into outer space to explain our humanity to curious aliens. On being asked what artefact he would place in the space rocket that would explain humanity to the aliens who found it in a distant galaxy, the biologist, Lewis Thomas, said, "I would vote for Bach, all of it – but that, of course, would be bragging!"

A note about music in space

In 1977, the *Voyager* space rocket took with it an audio record of sounds that it was felt represented the planet Earth. This record was dubbed *The Voyager Golden Record*. These sounds, if decoded by an alien life form in a distant galaxy, will give an idea of what life is like on our planet. Unfortunately, it will take *Voyager* 40,000 years to get to the nearest star, so if this record is ever found – highly unlikely, given the relative size of space and the size of a record – people will probably be long gone. Certainly, you don't need to worry about it! The Golden Record is not an attempt to communicate with intelligent life – it is what it says it is – a *record*.

However, it's interesting to know how NASA chose to represent our 'home'. There are animal and bird sounds, and "Hello" in 55 languages. There are the sounds of whales, surf and thunder. And there is music.

What music did they send? There is Chuck Berry, Senegalese drumming, Indonesian gamelan, Louis Armstrong, and various ethnic and traditional songs.

Classical music is represented by: lots of Bach, some Beethoven, a Mozart opera, and Stravinsky.

How will this book help me?

This book will guide you through the labyrinth of classical music in a way that is easy to understand. It will give you information and listening skills to enable you to get enjoyment from classical music, including those pieces that people find noisy or horrible – pieces, in fact, that are often dismissed as "just not music".

It will also give you the confidence to listen in the first place.

Much is made these days of our so-called inability to concentrate on anything for very long. The apparent reduction in our concentration span is blamed on all kinds of cultural activities. We can only keep watching TV from one commercial break to the next; our children can only concentrate for long enough to kill fast-moving aliens on a computer screen; a pop song is as long as we can manage to listen; even if we're into classical music, we can only digest it in extracts.

But this is balderdash, in my opinion. A full piece of classical music will normally be between ten and sixty minutes long. If you can watch a feature film, you can listen to a symphony. If you can follow a modern television drama, your concentration level is more than adequate!

What pieces of music should I listen to?

Listen to anything and everything you can get hold of. The trick is to remember what you like and what you don't.

Keep a note of composers you like, and bits of music you like. If you like an extract from a piece of music you hear on the radio, for example, try to get hold of the whole piece. If you like a movement of a symphony, try to listen to the whole symphony.

In this book, I will begin each chapter with a list of pieces you might like to listen to in order to get more from the chapter, and at the end of each chapter there will be suggestions for further listening.

Treat pieces of music you like as your friends – listen to them more than once, go to some trouble for them.

★ ★ ★ ★ ★

Why listen to classical music anyway?

Music is pre-verbal. It communicates with us on a deep, fundamental level that stretches right back to the womb and right back to our stone-age ancestors. Western classical music represents humanity's musical thinking for the last thousand years. Musical thinking is different to all other forms of thinking – it is non-visual and emotionally intelligent. In the last hundred years it has embraced non-Western, non-European modes of expression and understanding, and it has used other forms of music, like folk music, religious chant and jazz.

Classical music specialises in feelings and emotions. It can summon these up, explore them and change them. It communicates across the centuries and across cultures. It has lasted because it communicates something that cannot be expressed in words and cannot be made visible in paint or stone.

I cannot say why you might want to listen to classical music, but I can say why I do:

- It gives me emotional experiences I don't get from anywhere else.
- It provides me with beauty, hope and triumph when I need it.
- It nourishes the invisible parts of me (you can call it 'soul' if you like).

- It can just be fun, or happy, or sad, or exciting.

- It takes me, in my imagination, to places and states-of-mind I have never been to before.

- It makes me feel somehow connected to my memories and the distant past.

- It also provides me with an opportunity to sit down with a cup of tea!

There is no 'should' or 'ought' about listening to classical music. Listen because you want to, because – like all music – it speaks about the unsayable, and shows us the unseeable.

Part One

Songs of Innocence and Experience

Chapter One:
Womb Music

"You are the music while the music lasts."
– T. S. Eliot

For this Chapter try listening to

- Michael Tippett's *Concerto for Double String Orchestra,* particularly the slow second movement. At this stage, just let it wash over you.

- J S Bach's *Concerto for Two Violins.* Again, concentrate on the slow movement.

Imagine. You are lying in the dark. It is very warm. Everything is perfect. You have no words with which to think, no memories to distract you. Everything is now.

Music is playing all around you. There is the relaxed drumbeat of a slow heart, the whoosh-whoosh of blood, the high, sustained note of dreaming neurons, and the perpetual gurgle of a digestive system. All is enveloping sound.

This was you before you were born, before you emerged into a world of pain, and bright lights.

Beethoven heard this music. Mozart heard it. I heard it. John Lennon heard it. We all heard it. What did it mean, and why can't we remember it?

The ears develop in the womb long before the eyes. We can hear before we can see. By week seven, an embryo has developed an outer and inner ear, with hearing and balancing mechanisms. This happens before the skeleton develops, before cartilage changes to bone. Eyes are not fully open until week thirty two.

Because of this, the English composer, Sir Michael Tippett, believed that music was special amongst all the other arts, in that it had a direct and primitive connection to the nervous system.

So, like everyone else, I heard music long before I knew what sound was. I heard this nine-month concert during the winter and spring of 1952. I didn't have much to do at the time, so I gave the music my almost undivided attention. It filled my entire being, and became inextricably linked to how I was feeling – to hunger and pain, to rest and contentment. After all, I had this nine-month symphony of sound to listen to and not a lot to see!

Some experts believe that this early development of hearing is one of the reasons that music seems to have such an emotional impact on us in later life.

It's strange, therefore, that none of us seem to remember the music we heard in the womb. That first piece of music would have been all about rhythm. There would be the regular slow beat of a sleeping body at night, that would make me feel dreamy and contented and warm; and there would be sudden, unexplained fast beatings of panic, accompanied by shots of adrenaline during daytime emergencies, that would make me react with fear and excitement. And movement.

I like to think of myself kicking my mum while dancing to an unknown rhythm!

As well as these familiar, relatively constant sounds of Mum's body-orchestra, there would have been those far-off sounds from outside, totally incomprehensible and strange, but imbued with feelings, because in my world how could they be imbued with anything else?

I'm fairly sure about the body-music I heard then. After all, we've all heard it, or something like it: the beatings of the heart, the pulsing of the blood, the gurgling of digestion. But the sounds from outside are pure conjecture, some familiar through repetition, some surprising and bewildering. Some sounds would have made me feel at home, and some sounds would have disorientated me.

Obviously, I would have heard human voices, some well known to me, some unknown. Occasionally, this would be a song, but mostly it would be speech. The human voice, singing alone or in chorus, can still touch a deep emotional chord in me, as though reaching out from the distant time of drums and blood.

★ ★ ★ ★ ★

We lived in Leicester, in the East Midlands, in an ordinary house in an ordinary street. My dad was a carpenter and joiner, so even in the womb I was probably used to the sound of a hammer.

But what was unusual was that my dad played the piano rather well.

This never seemed unusual to me as a small child. I had known no other kind of father. I know now what a huge contribution he made to my love of music, and I am grateful to him for that. He and his brother, my Uncle Harold, were passionate classical music listeners, and both of them played the piano. Where they got this talent from I never knew.

Both of them talked endlessly about music. Many of these

discussions were typically male – who are the ten greatest composers? Was Beethoven as great as Mozart? What is your favourite symphony? The answers never seemed to matter – it was all purely for the delight of talking about music.

My dad had a baby grand piano in the sitting room and it dominated the room. He would practise most nights, play hymns on a Sunday and carols at Christmas. He would play Beethoven, Mozart and Brahms, and I must have absorbed these sound vibrations while at my private concert in the womb.

Research conducted at the University of Florida seems to show that babies in the womb can hear music outside (*Science Daily*, 23 Jan 2004), though the high notes tend to get filtered out somewhat. However, the bass notes come thundering through to babies. So that stomach-thumping effect of a loud bass line at a rock concert might be stirring a primeval memory of the womb. Hence also, the hypnotic effect of much dance music, and our bodily response to those deep organ notes in church.

It came as no surprise to me when I read that babies after birth actually remember the music they heard in the womb. Dr Lamont of Leicester University showed, in 2001, on the BBC programme, *Child of our Time*, that babies could remember a particular piece of music heard in the womb, even if they didn't hear it again after birth for twelve months.

This study involved pregnant women playing a piece of music to their unborn babies for the last three months before birth. Before this study, it was generally thought that babies could only remember for a couple of months at the most, but these babies recognised, and showed a preference for, the piece of music they had heard in the womb, even though they had not heard it for twelve months.

So I came out into the world with some memory of music, and with a basic, wordless understanding of its effect on my body and emotions. I didn't have the words to describe this, to myself or to others, but in many ways that in itself was a musical lesson, for ultimately the experience of music is a visceral, wordless apprehension of rhythm and sound, that predates speech as the ear predates the eye or the vocal chords.

Who knows what the other sounds were that I heard. It's strange to think that all kinds of sounds and music could be lurking around in my deep memory. This is true, of course, for everyone.

In no way am I suggesting for a moment that when I emerged howling into the world that the midwife said something along the lines of, "You know, just then I could've sworn that sounded like Beethoven's Fifth Symphony!" My memory of music just meant that I had heard music and had felt its power. Nearly all babies have felt this in some form, and in that sense we all come into the world, in Wordsworth's words, *"trailing clouds of glory"*.

So – to recap – when I emerged into this completely new and different universe we call the world, a little prematurely but nevertheless screaming and red of face, what wordless knowledge about sound did I bring with me? This knowledge would not have been very different from anyone else's, and it would influence my early understanding of the organised sound we call music.

Your 'womb music' will not have been exactly the same as mine. It may have been reggae, or rock, or Frank Sinatra. It really doesn't matter. Whatever the musical stimulation, you will have felt an umbilical pull. Early on in your embryonic life your brain was programmed to respond to all types and styles of music.

One of the basic elements of both music and speech that you would have absorbed before birth was a sense of pattern. You would have heard countless English sentences. Each one had its own pattern, but, taken as a whole, they would have followed a musical pattern. Nearly all of them would have risen upwards from the beginning to the middle of the sentence, then would have faded away to the final full stop.

This return to a sense of home is the heart of the musical experience. It is how we can feel when a tune has finished, and it is why we feel satisfied at the end of a piece of music. It is part of the reason why some music feels 'right' and complete.

My Womb Music didn't include any orchestral music, as far as I know, but many years later I can hear that sense of a familiar, arching language all over the place in music. For example, if you listen to the slow movement in Tippet's *Concerto for Double String Orchestra*, the melody soars upwards to a *caesura*, or break, such as we get in many English sentences, and particularly in Shakespeare – "*To be, or not to be, that is the question.* The caesura here is at the second comma. We pause here momentarily, before we descend to the full stop. We know we are at the end of a unit of thought – to check this, just try to stop after the word, *that*. Obviously, it doesn't make sense, but it doesn't sound right, either. If it were a foreign language, you would still know it was incomplete.

This happens in the same way in music. A simple melody like *Twinkle, Twinkle, Little Star* (composed, incidentally, by Mozart), rises to a caesura after 'star' and falls to the home note after 'are'. The line of music could not finish anywhere else.

The melody in Tippett's slow movement uses the same language. It climbs to the caesura, and then descends to the full stop, which in musical terms is called the home note, or tonic. We have an unconscious recognition of the musical meaning of the word, *key*.

Tippet's melody is beautiful and sounds to me to be very personal. It is like a solo voice singing to me in the womb.

Another piece of music that feels like this is the slow

movement of the *Concerto for Two Violins* by J S Bach. Here, the two violins twist together in a sinuous, non-competitive conversation. This kind of twining counterpoint makes me think of braided hair, or Celtic crosses, or the leaves and branches of a William Morris design, or the delicate patterns of pea tendrils and convolvulus. In a way, it is like being closely loved, curled in the arms of a lover or a mother.

This technique of composition, where two or more lines of music twist round each other, is known as 'counterpoint'. It is one of the most common techniques in classical music in all centuries, and it requires us to hear two melodies simultaneously. This is not as difficult as it sounds! The adjective to describe something as counterpoint is *contrapuntal*.

Also in these early years, I loved nursery rhymes and simple poetry. The music here was not just in the tunes, but also in the rhythm of the words, the rhyming sounds and repetition. All the words were right as a whole thing – you couldn't change a single word and it still sound right. There was completeness to a rhyme that was similar to a completeness in a melody or a chord in music. It's why, I suppose, I can remember them after fifty years.

Everybody can remember nursery rhymes and song lyrics from long ago, even when the words themselves make no sense. Why on earth can I remember things like these opening words from *The Jabberwocky* by Lewis Carroll?

"Twas brillig, and the slithy toves
 Did gyre and gimble in the wabe"?

I have deliberately not looked up this quotation from Lewis Carroll, because I wanted to know if I could, indeed, recall it. It may not be perfectly accurate, but I still think it's pretty good after forty years. I wish I could remember this morning's shopping list as well!

Music doesn't seem to improve non-musical memory, but certainly there is something about musical patterns that help us remember the music itself. Songs are relatively easy to remember, and I'm constantly amazed by my nearly word-perfect recall of pop songs I haven't heard or thought about for absolutely ages.

★ ★ ★ ★ ★

On the 17th December 1958, when I was six years old, my dad passed his piano exam to become an Associate of the London College of Music. This allowed him to put ALCM after his name, an unusual qualification for a chippy on a building site! It must have been a really big thing for him, but I don't remember it at all, and he never spoke of it to me.

This, of course, was right at the beginning of my journey through music, but, because of this exam, the house must have been full of piano music every day, as my dad wrestled with and practised his pieces. I don't remember the music, but I must have absorbed the difference between a difficult passage, and one that was relatively easy; between music played with feeling, with a *singing tone,* and that played mechanically, with too much thinking; and that creating and listening to music required perseverance and hard work.

Because it was a grand piano, I could crawl underneath it, make it into a bit of a den. I would be able to see Dad's feet on the loud and soft pedals, while above me the notes danced and reverberated. As a place to hide it was beyond compare. But it really came into its own as a place in which to think or daydream.

It was under that piano that I made acquaintance with a lot of music, in particular Chopin, Beethoven, and Debussy. To hear a Nocturne by Chopin still takes me back there, to the dusty smell of wood and carpet, and the vibration of bass chords. I just let it wash over me.

Beethoven seemed different to Chopin. It wasn't the kind of music that just flowed over me. I could hear the struggle in this music. Dad struggled to play it, but somehow I didn't feel that was where the struggle was. In difficult pieces of Chopin, what I heard was that it was difficult for the player. But with Beethoven, I would imagine the composer, struggling to say what he wanted to say. I didn't know what he wanted to say, but I knew it had nothing to do with words, and that the meaning lay purely within the sounds and the way they were organised.

It was my first lesson in musical style.

Much later, I heard a story which gave me some understanding of this. After the old and respected Haydn had heard the first performance of Beethoven's Third Symphony, he complained that, "Before this symphony music has been about music; this music is about the composer." After Beethoven music would never be the same again.

The struggle I was hearing was, I guess, Beethoven's struggle to express himself, to reveal the wordless part of his existence to the world. It was music as therapy.

And it can work for the listener as well!

When I was very young, I used to think that everyone was introduced to music under pianos! When I got older, I began to discover that no-one I knew had experienced this. I discovered my friends couldn't talk about Beethoven, and thought me a bit odd for doing so.

All children want to be like their friends, and I was saved by The Shadows and The Beatles, both of whom I listened to avidly. Radio Luxembourg provided me with my small talk at school.

This was the social side of shared music. With classical music, the sharing bit is quite difficult. I discovered that, while I had been communicating with Beethoven, I was not communicating with my friends. Classical music listeners tend not to talk about their music. Maybe it's time to come out of the closet!

At that time, some people had battery-driven record players, using six batteries, and producing a slowly dying sound as they ran out of charge. There was a local 'beatnik' who used to take his portable record player to the park and sit on the grass, playing Buddy Holly records. We kids thought this was wonderful, and followed him there. He was like the Pied Piper! Music became a social thing, and a way of feeling part of a group.

Pop music was the 'glue' that held groups of people together. It has always been successful at that, at celebrating and communicating differences and similarities. Pop music is built largely on the idea of the 'in' and 'out' crowd, the 'hip' and 'unhip'.

Communication and community have the same linguistic root. When I was a teenager, I felt that I straddled two communities; but that seemed a richness, not a problem. It still is a richness.

Suggestions for Further Listening

- If you liked **Tippett**, you might like **Britten**.
- If you liked **Bach**, you might like **Handel**.

Chapter Two:
Songs of Innocence
The Music of Childhood

*"Music expresses that which cannot be said and on which
it is impossible to be silent."*
−Victor Hugo

For this Chapter try listening to

- Beethoven's *Moonlight Sonata* for piano.

- Mendelssohn's *Hebrides Overture*, often known as *Fingal's Cave.*

- Elgar's *Nimrod*, which is part of his *Enigma Variations.*

The Moonlight Sonata – Beethoven

Many times have I crawled under the piano to listen to my dad practise and play Beethoven's *Moonlight Sonata*. He even taught me to roughly follow the notes in the score so I could turn the pages for him, which made me feel very important.

The Moonlight Sonata is one of the most widely known pieces of classical music. Nearly everyone knows it, or thinks they do. It is a European cultural icon, like the *Mona Lisa*. And it has suffered immeasurably as a result.

The first thing to realise is that it has absolutely nothing to do with moonlight; and probably at no point during its composition was Beethoven trying to describe moonlight. Why, after all, would he want to do that on a piano?

Composers, of course, do try to describe things in music. Music that tries to do this is called *programme music*. However, this was mainly done by composers after Beethoven's time – in Beethoven's day musicians generally left physical description to artists and writers. Most people before Beethoven and during his time considered that music dealt with non-physical things, like music itself, or harmony, or mathematics, or emotions, or God and religion.

Beethoven never called this music the *Moonlight Sonata* – he called it *Sonata Number 14*. It was later editors of the sheet music, with an ear for a snappy title, who called it *The Moonlight*.

"What is a piano sonata?" It is an extended piece for solo piano, generally in three movements, or sections. You can see these movements like the chapters of a book, and you have to read all of them. You wouldn't dream of reading one chapter and saying you knew the book – the same is true of music.

A strange thing you'll notice at classical concerts is that the audience doesn't applaud at the end of Movements. This is because the music hasn't finished. Music is born out of silence and returns to silence at the end, and these silences are, in a way, part of the music as well as the sounds. In an important sense, the symphony, or sonata, or whatever, is still going on in the gaps between movements. When you applaud at the end of a play, or at the end of the music, the spell is broken – you become yourself again, the performers become tellers of stories, the emotions are dissipated, and you are back in an audience in a hall. So those moments of silence before, in and after the music are important. They allow you to absorb the emotion and to prepare for a change.

The *Moonlight* was composed in 1801, when two significant things were happening to Beethoven.

The first thing was that he had fallen in love with one of his aristocratic piano students, the Countess Julia Guicciardi, who was sixteen when she had first become his pupil.

Unfortunately, he was not of her social class, and, although Beethoven believed she loved him, in 1803 she married Count Gullenberg. After Beethoven's death, she recalled him as "very ugly, but noble, refined in feeling and culture." Nevertheless, the sonata is dedicated to her, and his feelings for her come through much more strongly than any spurious ones about moonlight.

The other significant factor was his increasing awareness of his early deafness. His family was poor, and he depended on his teaching, piano playing and conducting for his livelihood. There were no royalties or lucrative film deals in 1801!

So there really couldn't have been anything worse for someone like Beethoven than impending deafness. The prognosis was awful – incurable and eventual total deafness. No wonder the popular idea of him is bad-tempered and frustrated!

(This view of Beethoven's personality is a bit of a myth, actually. Sometimes he was grumpy and bad-tempered, but who isn't? Even those of us who have nothing very much to be grumpy about? He was a popular man in the Vienna coffee houses of his day, and when he died, thousands of people turned out for his funeral. Maybe the grumpy myth was invented to account for the wildness of his hairstyle!)

When we know about his fear of deafness, and his

disappointment in love, *The Moonlight Sonata* gains an emotional impact far beyond the popular picture view of the piece.

The famous First Movement seems to me a love letter to Julia. I know this will be considered fanciful, and it certainly wasn't how I heard it when I was under the piano in Leicester, but I can just imagine him playing it to his pupil sitting beside him at the piano, watching for signs of understanding.

What is a key?

Most music is in a particular key – the key of C major, for example – and this makes it feel like the music has a home, a note or chord on which it feels finished. In the key of C major, for example, the notes used would be the notes in the C major scale (C D E F G A B), and it would feel finished on the note of C. Similarly, a piece in the key of E would use the notes of the E scale (E F sharp G sharp A B C sharp D sharp) and would feel finished on E.

If you have access to a piano or keyboard, go and play a random series of white notes (no black notes allowed). Try to hear it as a tune. Keep playing till it sounds like the end. This last note will be a C, because you have only used notes in the C scale. Go on – try it.

Now do the same thing, but this time only with the black notes. This time, the tune will sound finished on F sharp, because these notes are all in the scale of F sharp.

If you want to know what key a piece of music is in, listen to the end and hold the last note in your head. Go to the piano and find that note – that is the key. This is not 100% accurate, because composers like to break the rules, but it's a good guide.

Most people don't realise there is more to the *Moonlight* than that famous First Movement, beautiful though it is.

If the *Moonlight* was just this movement, then the later title given to it might just about make sense. But there is more. As a result, the true power of this piece of music is missed.

The Second Movement changes the mood to a dance. It is light and happy, and a little flirtatious. But it doesn't say 'moonlight' to me.

But the mood doesn't stay in that sociable, slightly frivolous vein. Beethoven introduces a feeling of doubt and uncertainty by changing key. This is called *modulation*.

Modulation is a crucial tool for composers, because it introduces conflict and drama.

Sometimes, a composer changes key within a piece of music. This happens in pop songs, too, but classical music may change key several times, and the changes are rarely sudden and obvious. You can hear that the music is modulating by its sense of rootlessness and it sounds as if it is somehow slipping and sometimes slightly out of tune.

This is exploited by composers to make the music dramatic, to help it express conflict, change, doubt, and movement.

In this particular case, it undermines the lightness and happiness of the dance. It is as though he has doubts about the reality of this relationship with the Countess.

The third and final movement is the one that turns the world of the First Movement on its head. It explodes from the end of the Second Movement with anger and violence. It is the very opposite of the tranquillity of the famous beginning, and that opposition is the whole point of *The Moonlight Sonata*.

When I followed the music for the last movement as a boy, I was always amazed at how many notes there were, and at how quickly I had to turn the pages. How could my father, with his workman's hands and his right thumb that had been broken, be so fast and nimble? These fast bits are obviously difficult to play, but my dad also taught me that the real skill of a musician was to play the slow lyrical bits with beautiful tone. This requires grace and artistry and sensitivity, rather than mere technical virtuosity.

This transition between the second and third movements of the *Moonlight Sonata* is a good example of why audiences don't applaud between movements. If you applauded the Second Movement, there would be no silence, and therefore no shock when the Third Movement began. We tend to forget that music comes out of silence and returns to silence. That silence is part of the experience – the silence out of which an infinite number of possibilities emerge, and the silence to which everything returns.

The Third Movement of *The Moonlight Sonata* is an angry tumble of notes. Here is the anger of a passionate man rejected in love, and the anger and fear of someone losing the sense that made the world understandable. As the movement progresses it gets angrier, until the music seems to explode with the tension into a cascade of percussive notes. It's almost as though Beethoven has ripped the tune apart.

Interestingly, this style of playing would not have been possible before Beethoven, because the design and engineering of the piano itself would not have been able to withstand it. With physical improvements in the piano as an instrument, Beethoven could compose in this angry, percussive style.

So at the end we realise that this music is not just about the famous bit at all. It is about the emotional movement from sentimental feelings of love and quietness, to violence and frustration. Only if we listen to the whole Sonata can we go through that experience with Beethoven.

★ ★ ★ ★ ★

I Go To Junior School

The next phase of my musical education was at junior school. Those lessons formally described as Music were taught in a separate building, called the Hut. This is indeed what it was like – wooden walls, cold in winter, hot in summer.

Lessons were of two kinds: singing, and playing. In singing lessons we all sang pretend folk songs, like *The Gentleman Soldier;* playing lessons involved getting 'The Instruments' out, and playing pieces of music, like an orchestra. The instruments were all, as far as I can recall, from the percussion family – drums, tambourines, triangles, castanets, cymbals, and so on.

But what also happened at that school was something private and peripheral.

Every morning, as the various classes gathered in the school hall for morning Assembly, the Head Teacher would play classical music on the school's standard-issue brown record player.

On the wall was a handwritten notice, which read, "This week's composer", and under it would be posted the composer of the music we were assembling to that week.

It became a secret game in my head. As my class came down the stairs to the hall, I could hear the music, and I would try to guess the composer's name. In this way, I learned to recognise the music, and sometimes the style, of a number of composers: Mozart, Handel, Grieg, Brahms, Elgar, and others.

Two pieces of music, featured in This Week's Composer in Assembly, affected me particularly. They were *Fingal's Cave* by Mendelssohn, and *Nimrod* by Elgar.

'Fingal's Cave' – Mendelssohn

Fingal's Cave may have been the first piece of orchestral music I recognised by name. It was written in 1829, and the name by which musicians know it is *The Hebrides Overture*. Overtures are pieces of music played at the beginning of something, like an opera. In stage musicals, they tend to be made up of extracts and material from the whole musical, but in classical music they can, and often do, stand alone. Many of them are concert pieces, and are usually played at the beginning of classical concerts. This is true of *Fingal's Cave*.

Felix Mendelssohn was born in Hamburg in 1809, and was only 38 when he died. He was born into a wealthy banking family, and spent much time travelling throughout Europe. These travels often resulted in music inspired, directly or indirectly, by the places he visited. Thus, we have *The Hebrides Overture*, the *Italian Symphony*, and the *Scottish Symphony*.

The Hebrides was inspired by a boat trip Mendelssohn took to view the sea cave, known as Fingal's Cave, on the Isle of Staffa. It is a remarkable geological feature, geologically connected to the Giant's Causeway in County Antrim, and the name of the cave in Gaelic is lovely – it translates as 'The Cave of Melody'.

The cave is only accessible by boat, and it was admired by nineteenth century artists other than Mendelssohn – Turner painted it, for example, and Keats wrote about it in 1818, and called it, "This cathedral of the sea."

Many pieces of classical music appear to paint pictures. Some examples would be Richard Strauss's *Alpine Symphony*, *In the South* by Elgar, or *Symphonia Antarctica* by Vaughan Williams. *Fingal's Cave* is one of these.

I have a problem with this, however. It seems to suggest that, if you don't know the title, the music would be impossible to 'understand', or that if you don't know what Fingal's Cave looks like you won't know if it is a good picture or even a good piece of music.

Of course, like any artist in any medium, composers are often inspired by visual stimuli, particularly landscapes. But what they then communicate through their music is not the precise colour or visual placement of objects, but the feelings and emotions and imaginings that the landscape inspires in them.

All music can stimulate pictures in your imagination. It would be strange if it didn't. However, there are no right pictures. Your pictures, if any, are simply your response to the music in non-verbal terms; in a way, it constitutes your side of the communication between you and the composer.

If it had been really important to Mendelssohn that he communicated visually, he would have learned to be a painter, not a composer. This music is a wordless depiction of his feelings at the time, and so we can still imagine the long swells of the sea and their breaking, but I don't believe anyone would know it was about a sea cave if the title didn't tell us.

Luckily, when I heard *Fingal's Cave* in those far-off days, I didn't know what Fingal's Cave was. The music could have been called anything and I still would have liked it, it still would have 'meant' the same to me.

The idea that music in some way means a place or a picture can be a real problem for a listener. Of course, the visit to Fingal's Cave and the emotions it created provided the inspiration for Mendelssohn, and in that sense it's interesting, but it is not essential to an understanding of the music, and it certainly shouldn't prevent us from listening to it in any other way.

So what did it mean to me back then?

This is really difficult to talk about, because music is not a 'word thing'. But it must have meant **something** to me.

I think I can sum it up in the word, 'surge'.

I didn't play an instrument, and I didn't know the instruments of a classical orchestra. So I couldn't respond as a musician, and I couldn't respond to the blending of the different instruments, otherwise known as orchestration, wonderful though it is in *Fingal's Cave*.

But I could hear the slow build-up of sound, and the sense of inevitability and power behind each surge. It could have been the sea, or the wind, or a feeling of vertigo, but, whatever you see, what I felt is a calm power outside myself, a feeling of being enveloped and lifted like a boat on a long swell, but at the same time a feeling that it was controlled, that everything was finely graded.

It has become so natural for us to think that meaning has to be expressed in words that we are sometimes puzzled by what music 'means'. When someone asks me what a piece of music means, I know I don't help much when I say vague things like, "It just means what it sounds like." I know people want 'word answers', like, "Shostakovich is about the attempt of the individual to find expression in a totalitarian state." But how would that help you to listen to his Fifth Symphony?

This is all very strange, I know, but the precise way of talking about these things is to play the music. No more, no less. When you listen to the opening of *Fingal's Cave* don't worry about what it means. Just listen carefully to it and allow images to come into your mind. There are no right images – it might be the sea, or it might be a colour. Or it might be nothing – just an enjoyment of the tune, or a desire to sway.

'Nimrod' – Elgar

Nimrod, by Edward Elgar, had a different significance for me.

In 1962 the family got a portable, battery-driven record player. This meant that my older sister could join the new record library in Leicester. Borrowed records were carried in a special cardboard carrier, with "Goldsmith's Record Library" printed on the side. My sister told me it was quite a status symbol in the town!

One day she brought home Elgar's *Enigma Variations* from the library. *Nimrod* is the name given to one of the variations – it is part of a bigger piece of music, although I didn't know this at the time.

She was listening to it with Dad, when I walked into the room. *Nimrod* started to play, and I knew it from school. I remember the music made me cry, and my sister laughed at me. Immediately, Dad said, "Leave him alone. It's all right for him to cry." I've never ceased to be grateful to him for that interjection – I absorbed the two messages, that it was all right for boys to cry, and a recognition that music could, indeed **should**, deeply touch our emotions.

It was a bit of a shock to me to discover that *Nimrod* was just a part of something else and not complete in itself. It was not a particularly large section of a piece of music called, "*Theme and Variations on an Original Theme (Enigma)*", composed by Elgar in 1899. It is known simply as *The Enigma Variations*.

Theme and Variations is a musical form, like Symphony, Sonata or Overture. It consists of a theme, or melody, which the composer then repeats in varied ways; some so varied they are almost unrecognisable. The composer might play the theme quicker, or slower, with different instruments, or in a different rhythm. Apart from the basic pleasure to be gained from the sound of the music (assuming that it is pleasurable, in some way!), the interest lies in how cleverly and inventively the composer has varied the theme.

Elgar was forty-two when he wrote this music. Before this he was only known to a small audience around his native Worcester, but it was *The Enigma Variations* that gave him national fame. Outside England he is still not particularly well known, and if you go abroad *The Enigma Variations* is probably the only music by Elgar that anyone, including musicians, will have heard of. When I went to St Petersburg after the fall of the Soviet Union, I took recordings of other works by Elgar to give as presents to musicians at the Conservatoire, who knew nothing of him.

For many people he is the quintessential English composer, the composer of *Land of Hope and Glory*, an Edwardian gentleman with a moustache and a bicycle. All those rosy, nostalgic images accrue to him and his music – long summers, the British Empire, village cricket, the Cotswolds, picnic hampers and straw boaters; so much so, that composers of the next generation, scarred by the First World War, sneeringly described it as "English cowpat music".

None of these images, positive or negative, help us to understand his music, although they probably go some way towards explaining the lack of interest in his music outside England.

The Enigma Variations consists of, as you would expect from the full title, a theme written by Elgar at the beginning, followed by fourteen variations, of which *Nimrod* is one. He dedicated it "To friends pictured within". I wish he hadn't, because it has diverted attention from the music itself ever since.

The initials of someone Elgar knew head each variation, and the variation is a kind of portrait in music of each friend. Some of these musical portraits are almost impossible for the average listener to spot – the one depicting Elgar himself, for example, uses a tune that Elgar used to whistle on his bicycle as he was nearing home. People have seen this as a cryptic puzzle, and tried to work out who the friends were. If this interests you, I must tell you that they have all been identified! You will be able to find their names in the notes of most recordings.

The Enigma Variations is delicately scored (*scoring* is the term given to the number and type of instruments), and has the feel of a landscape watercolour. In that way, I suppose, it is part of an English tradition. Its melodies all seem to be like arches, climbing upwards and hovering at the apex. Put together, they seem to create a Gothic cathedral of flying buttresses and vaulting roof.

As a child, images of Gothic cathedrals would have meant nothing. What I heard was a piece of music that made my throat swell and my eyes cry even though I didn't feel sad. Only music could do this. What I learned is that an extract from a piece of music, like a movement, or a favourite bit, did not mean the same on its own as it did when it was heard in its full musical context.

Imagine, for example, a picture of someone waving a Union Jack. That picture alone might stir something in you, and you might interpret it in a certain way. Widen the view, though, and you might see that the holder of the flag is a young man at the Last Night of the Proms. Maybe the meaning of the picture has changed. Or the retreating lens might reveal that the flag is about to be burned in a war-torn country – the same image with a different meaning again.

So it is with music. A slow movement played as though it was a complete piece, might be relaxing and gentle. But when flanked by other movements, with different emotional impacts, it might just be a temporary and forlorn haven, or it might be ironic or serve to increase tension.

So, if you are struggling to 'understand' classical music, try to listen to entire works, not just extracts or movements. These extracts do not contain the meaning of the music, any more than a single chapter has the meaning of a novel

My second piece of advice is to listen carefully. Don't listen to it as background music.

And finally, don't worry about meaning. It's music, not an elaborate form of morse code!

Suggestions for Further Listening

- If you liked **Beethoven**, you might like **Schubert**.
- If you liked **Mendelssohn**, you might like **Bruch**.
- If you liked **Elgar**, you might like **Vaughan Williams**.

Chapter Three:
Playing the Orchestra
And Falling in Love

"God tells me how the music should sound, but you stand in the way"
– Arturo Toscanini to a trumpet player

For this Chapter try listening to

- *Finlandia* by Sibelius.

- Finale of Mahler's *Symphony No. 8*, known as *Symphony of a Thousand*.

When my dad realised I was interested in listening to classical music, but not in playing it, he didn't push me to play the piano. I think this was probably right at the time – it would not have been easy for him to be strict with me and I really didn't fancy all those scales and arpeggios!

As I entered my teenage years I chose to play the guitar, and returned to the piano as an adult. Instead, Dad encouraged my interest by taking me to see Walt Disney's *Fantasia*, where I was introduced to the exciting new sound worlds of Bach and Stravinsky. He also took me to occasional classical concerts at the De Montfort Hall in Leicester.

The first concert I remember going to was the Finnish Radio Orchestra, playing a programme of the Finnish composer, Sibelius. I became lost in music that transported me to a world of snow and endless forest.

Concert seats were not cheap, so we would queue for the unreserved ones. These were benches set on stage at the back of the orchestra, with a perfect view of the audience and the conductor, a distorted sound balance, and a wonderful chance to get to know the french horns, percussion, or trombones, as these instruments are usually placed at the back of the orchestra.

Because we went to concerts, and because we sat where we did, there was much discussion of conductors between my father, my uncle and myself. Great conductors like Barbirolli and Boult were almost family friends, and Dad and Uncle talked in hushed tones of Toscanini and Thomas Beecham. I realised early on that these Bohemian-looking old men were doing something rather special, but at that age I wasn't sure what it was.

Conductors

What exactly does a conductor of an orchestra do? He (it is usually a man, even today) is obviously recognised by orchestra and audience as important. Conductors of the past are spoken of with reverence — names like Toscanini, Furtwangler and Klemperer. Even in my own time, conductors have achieved, or been given, almost legendary status, like Karajan and Solti. The name *conductor* is interesting, because it suggests a direct link, or channel, between the composer and the orchestra.

Musicians and writers still use the word *maestro* to address conductors, and they don't seem to have their tongues in their cheeks at the time!

At concerts, audiences applaud the conductor when he comes on stage, before he has actually done anything. Even the orchestra doesn't get that – they just seem to slink on in dribs and drabs, as though they are hoping no one will see them.

I'm not talking about the 1930s here, I'm talking about the 1960s, the decade of disrespect, when the Establishment supposedly fell to its knees before the high altar of satire, the Peace Movement and Rock and Roll. It didn't happen like that with orchestral conductors.

So what do they do to deserve such accolades?

At the most basic level, they beat time for the musicians. All the players in the orchestra are reading the same music, but to keep them all playing at the same tempo requires someone outside with the authority to be able to say, "It goes at **this** speed."

Before the nineteenth century, someone would stand at the front and bang a stick on the flor – literally *beat* time. This was the cause of the only known example of death-by-conducting! The seventeenth century conductor, Jean-Baptiste Lully, stabbed himself in the foot with his staff and died when it went gangrenous.

Later the stick would become the conductor's baton. The only purpose of the baton is to extend the movement of the conductor's arm, so that the brass players at the back can see it.

Different conductors take the same piece of music at different speeds, so don't expect all performances of your favourite piece of music to sound the same. Composers give guidelines, of course, but it is not an exact science. It **could** be, of course – the tempo of a piece could be given very precisely and scientifically, and a metronome could be placed in front of the orchestra.

However, it wouldn't sound like music. It would lack the flow and flexibility of the real thing.

Conductors approach music as though it were alive. I once heard the conductor, Ricardo Chailly talk about the importance of what he called *elasticity* in conducting, and Brian Pollard, bassoonist in the Concertegebouw Orchestra of Amsterdam, in an interview about conducting, describes the sense of time within an orchestra as a flow:

"It is fluid and imprecise. If you put on the metronome at the same time as the music, the metronome gets in front, or it gets behind." He describes time in an orchestra as "All waves. It's building up, it's going down; it's getting more tense, it's relaxing, then the tension builds again. And all these waves have different measures, different sizes, and they're going at different speeds. The conductor has to help the orchestral players with this."

Some conductors take this fluidity further than others. Wilhelm Furtwangler, for example, was famous in his day for not being clear about the beat. Precision in timing was not as important for him as what he may have called the 'fluid soul' of the music. In fact, he stormed out of a Toscanini concert once, shouting, "Bloody time beater!"

You can imagine, then, how difficult it is for an orchestra of maybe 100 musicians to play together. Not only do they all have to go at the same speed, but they all have to be elastic at the same time and in the same way.

Another major concern of the conductor is the control of sound balance. He has to make sure that the audience can hear every instrument, every note. For example, he has to ensure that we can hear the solo soprano in the Finale of Mahler's *Symphony of a Thousand*, singing at the same time as two huge symphony orchestras, a grand organ and two full choirs.

A Note on Orchestras

In the past, orchestras were composed of local musicians. Even in most of the twentieth century, the musicians in the Berlin Philharmonic would have been almost exclusively German, the Leningrad Philharmonic would have had Russian players, the Royal Philharmonic, English players, and so on. As a result, orchestras took on a kind of national identity, a characteristic way of playing and a distinctive approach to music-making. Thus, an English orchestra would 'have a feel for' Elgar, a German one for Brahms, a Russian one for Tchaikovsky, and so on.

Particular orchestras developed close and creative ties with particular conductors. Examples of this are: Barbirolli and the Halle, Boult and the London Philharmonic, Furtwangler and the Berlin Philharmonic, Toscanini and the NBC (National Broadcasting Company) Symphony Orchestra (which, incidentally, was created especially for Toscanini), Reiner and the Boston Symphony. The list is very long.

When a conductor's strength and interest marries with an appropriate orchestra, we get great performances and recordings, such as the Leningrad Orchestra playing Tchaikovsky under the baton of Evgeny Mravinsky.

Things are changing, however. In the search for all-round excellence, orchestras hire musicians from all over the place. It is like Premiership football! As a result, the leading orchestras are beginning to sound the same and are losing their characteristic sounds.

Modern digital recording, however, means that it is rare to get an orchestra with a 'bad' sound, or even a different one. So, if you are looking to buy a modern recording of a work, just look for a well-known orchestra.

This is Mahler at his most over the top, but the volume balance must be perfectly controlled.

When you watch a conductor at work, you will notice that he is constantly making adjustments to sound levels with his left hand (the one without the baton).

To sum up, then: the instrument is the orchestra, and the player is the conductor. He plays the orchestra with his arms and eyes. Some conductors, like Bernstein, use their entire bodies; some stand almost expressionless yet full of brooding intensity, like Richard Strauss, whose rule was that conductors should never perspire!

The last word on the subject of conducting can go to the great German conductor and friend of Mahler, Bruno Walter, who said: "If the conductor is of warm heart and of sincerity, the musicians will listen to him. But if he does not love nature, if he loves not the brook and the woods, how can he conduct Beethoven's *Pastoral Symphony*? If he feels not love and ecstasy, how can he conduct Wagner's *Tristan und Isolde*?"

★ ★ ★ ★ ★

Falling in Love

When my parents bought our first record player, my dad also bought a little collection of LP records. Because we didn't have many, the few we had were really precious, and I got to know every note through constant playing.

I can remember the performances even now: Schubert's *Great C major* Symphony, conducted by Toscanini; Beethoven's *Eroica* Symphony and Tchaikovsky's *Pathetique* Symphony, both conducted by Adrian Boult, *Scheherezade* (I loved the name!) by

Rimsky Korsakov; Beethoven's fourth and fifth Piano Concertos, with the piano played by Solomon; and Beethoven's Violin Concerto, played by Yehudi Menuhin.

I bought myself a couple of classical records from the little supermarket at the end of the road. They were on the Music for Pleasure label, and they cost 13/6, or 62p. The first one I bought was a collection of overtures, including *Fingal's Cave* and Tchaikovsky's *1812* Overture, celebrating the Russian defeat of Napoleon in 1812. Because I liked *Fingal's Cave*, I next bought Mendelssohn's *Italian Symphony*, with Schubert's *Unfinished Symphony* on the other side.

I can clearly remember the record sleeves, and that the sleeve for Schubert's *Unfinished*, which was a photograph of the reflection in a lake, never looked right because it always looked upside down, even when you knew it was a reflection!

These first records provided me with definitive performances. Any other recordings of these pieces I have listened to since, seem poor in comparison. This is not because they were particularly brilliant performances – some of them were, some weren't – but because they were the first ones with which I became familiar. I still judge subsequent performances against them.

When I was about fourteen, I joined the record library in town, and then I, too, could carry the Goldsmith Record Library cardboard carrier, that marked me out as a music lover, and therefore very sophisticated!

That library was the most wonderful thing. It had hundreds of classical records, and I could take any of them home for a week for the equivalent of 2p. Here was my musical university, and, because I could only have a record for a week, I would play it constantly for the whole week, so that, by the time I took it back, I was almost note-perfect in my recall.

I didn't work through the library in any organised fashion. If

I liked it, I would get more by the same composer. If I didn't like it, I still had only that record to play for the week, and I discovered that as I got to know it, I grew to like it.

Most new music is difficult at first. It is like a foreign language – at first you can't distinguish a single word, but eventually your ear becomes tuned in, and the music reveals itself coyly, bit by bit, as if worried you might not appreciate it.

Every week I would bring home my new record to show my dad, like some pack animal bringing a kill back to the den. Dad enjoyed this process as much as I did and, although he would talk with me about the music, and would sometimes explain on the piano technical bits in the sleeve notes I didn't understand, he never interfered with the meandering route of my journey.

I had encountered the Finnish composer Sibelius at my first concert. Maybe that early experience had sown a seed, but when I stumbled on Sibelius's symphonies in the library, I reacted as though something had exploded inside me. It felt as though I had discovered my very own composer. It was almost like falling in love.

I started with his First Symphony, and worked through them in order. There are seven in all. I listened to anything else by him that I could get my hands on. I bought recordings of the symphonies, on the Decca Eclipse cheap label, all of which were conducted by Anthony Collins, and I read about the man and his music, and about Finland.

I think that everyone has his or her own Sibelius somewhere. For a friend of mine, it was Bartock; for another, it was Beethoven. It doesn't matter who is going to knock your musical socks off, but somebody will, and that music is out there already. Go find it.

Suggestions for Further Listening

- If you liked **Sibelius**, you might like **Shostakovich**.
- If you liked **Mahler**, you might like **Saint-Saens**.

Chapter Four:
Songs of Experience
Expanding Horizons

"Music can change the world"
- Beethoven

For this Chapter try listening to

- *Symphony No.2* by Sibelius.

- *Tapiola* by Sibelius

- *Atmospheres for Orchestra* by Ligeti. This can also be found on the soundtrack for the film *2001*.

Sibelius

Sibelius was born in Finland in 1865. Finland didn't become independent from Russia until 1917, and the young Sibelius was very much a patriotic nationalist, writing music in the style of

Tchaikovsky. His early piece, *Finlandia*, which I had heard at my first concert, is an expression of this Nationalism – not because of its title, but because of the folk-inspired melodies and rhythms.

His early symphonies are very like Tchaikovsky, which is hardly surprising. I have known people who would consider this to be a criticism, because musical snobs are a bit sniffy about Tchaikovsky, considering his music to be sentimental and bombastic. It is true that great composers need to find their own voice. But everyone is influenced by someone early on in their careers, and Tchaikovsky is not such a bad start!

After his Third Symphony, Sibelius's music became more original, but still generally accessible. The music is still tonal (which means it still adheres to the traditional notion of music being in identifiable keys), and can be described as late or post-Romantic, but it has acquired a personality of its own. It tells of the landscape of the North, of cold and vast forests and huge mountain presences, of a hostile, or at least indifferent, Nature.

It is a spiritual view of the world that places human beings in a beautiful and huge landscape, and then watches them disappear into irrelevancy.

It massively appealed to the melancholia of a male adolescent!

Tapiola – Sibelius

I first encountered Sibelius's masterpiece, *Tapiola*, when my uncle lent me an old record of it, coupled with the Fourth Symphony, conducted by Otto Klemperer. It was a thick and heavy disc of vinyl, from Columbia Records.

It seems very 'geeky' now, but I was reading '*The Lord of the Rings*' at the time, and I couldn't put it down. So *Tapiola* became the background music for 'The Lord of the Rings', and the two works – the book and the music – became inextricably inter-meshed.

So, without knowing anything about the music, it came to represent to me the dark forests and mountains of Middle Earth, and a constant sense of threat. It became my favourite piece of music, although I would like to think my tastes are more catholic now.

Tapiola was the last piece of music of any consequence that Sibelius wrote. It heralded a thirty-year silence, and I feel that was because he had said everything he wanted to say in Tapiola, and after writing it the only thing left was silence. In the music he approaches a form of self-annihilation in the vastness of the Northern forests, where human activity is of no importance. The only thing left, after visiting such a place, was inscrutable quiet.

It was composed in 1926. Sibelius must have felt that the classical music world was becoming hostile to his style of music. It seemed as though the mainstream was following the route of Stravinsky and Schoenberg and Twelve-note Serialism (see later). This must have been a contributing factor to his self-imposed exile to the Finnish countryside.

The music of Tapiola is sparse and cold. Sibelius said that other composers were serving up cocktails, but he was offering us pure, cold water. This is the music of a glacier, sharp and cold and clear, and incredibly powerful. This glacial sharpness is often heard in Sibelius's music, particularly when he writes music for the strings that is almost painfully high and thin.

This is music that grows organically, like a tree, rather than by following a human structural pattern. This is only right, of course, when the subject matter is not human. The title gives away this subject matter, because 'Tapiola', in Finnish mythology is the realm of Tapio, the god of the forest.

Whenever you run up against the word 'forest' in relation to Sibelius, it's important to remember that we are not talking about a gentle English wood in June. This is a dark, brooding wilderness, with no place for human beings.

The organic nature of the music's growth means that we don't get movements or sections. The music starts very simply, like a seed, and develops out of that seed in one long piece. The seed contains within itself all that is necessary to produce the final structure.

It begins with this seed, a short theme in the strings, which seems to slip down a little scale. Behind it is a long clarinet note, which, after the seed theme has been repeated, continues and seems to grow out of the seed, bringing with it a sense of space and emptiness. It sounds as though the clarinet echoes and disappears into the vastness of the forest.

This is what *Tapiola* is all about. Everything is held within this limitless space. Short melodies echo and then disappear. To me, it seems as though, when something does emerge, it then loses its identity in the forest. There are periods of panic but eventually the music enters a hushed period, almost as if the forest had become the cathedral of god. Here the music rests for a while in a profound stillness that is the spiritual centre of the work.

It is in this part of the music that Sibelius seems to experience the 'otherness' of his Nature-God, and, as the work draws to a close, he experiences panic at the loss of the vision of Tapio. There is a remarkable piece of writing in the violins, in which the first and second violins play opposing scales. It sounds like wind in the trees. However, to me this scurrying sound is like panic, a state of grief about losing the vision he has had in the limitless forest.

After an experience as overwhelming as this, I suppose everything is an anti-climax, and it is almost like this for Sibelius himself. After this music he retired from public life and wrote very little. Some people believe he wrote a final symphony but burned it. We will never know.

Sibelius – Symphony No. 2

I remember hearing the Finale of Sibelius's Second Symphony for the first time. Symphonies usually consist of four movements, charting the development of a musical conflict or struggle. (I will return to the structure of a symphony later.) Sibelius runs the last two movements of this symphony together, so that the climax builds over a long time.

The themes, or tunes, emerge from the music in a way that is typical of Sibelius. They appear to be discovered lurking somewhere in the undergrowth of the orchestra, and then come out of hiding bit by bit. For the listener, this process is a series of realisations, dawnings, as you recognise that a fragment you heard a couple of minutes earlier, has grown into the beginning of a big tune.

This big tune will then fragment, falling apart as though Sibelius had decided it wasn't big enough, or powerful enough, to contain the majesty of mountains and the Northern landscape and his spiritual reaction to it. This results in a constant feeling of frustration for the listener, and the tension builds until the climax bursts into the music, and it feels as though we are flying.

For me, at sixteen, this was an amazing feeling. I had walked in high places in Scotland, the Peak District, and the Lakes, and no other music made me feel that sense of space and freedom that I had felt on the high fells.

Sibelius had well and truly got me!

Flowers in my hair

This was 1968 – what became known as *the summer of love*. It didn't quite get to Leicester, despite the rumours of *love-ins* in the park. But we did listen avidly to the music and dreamed of San Francisco. Some of my friends even set off to Kathmandu on the hippy trail to Enlightenment, although I don't think any of them actually got there.

I didn't just listen to Mozart, but I didn't stop listening to him either. I listened to the psychedelic rock of *Pink Floyd*, but I also listened to the avant-garde music of Stockhausen and Xenakis; I listened to the folk-rock of *Fairport Convention*, but also to the folk-inspired music of Vaughan Williams; to the jazz-influenced *Soft Machine*, but also Gershwin and Bernstein.

Rock and popular music were important to me, and I'm not making any kind of elitist judgement here. Popular music works in relatively short bursts. A popular song is like a snapshot, and has, therefore, an incredible ability to bring back memories of a particular time in your life. They are little packages of nostalgia. You can create an autobiography in popular song, which is why Dennis Potter could use it so effectively in his TV dramas.

Classical music doesn't do this. It tends to be too long, for a start, and so doesn't concern itself with a single emotion, mood or event. However much I've listened to classical music, very little of it has accumulated memories for me. It exists separately from me, outside me, and this is why it can take me to places and emotional states I have never been.

If I wanted to remember what it was like for me when I was sixteen or seventeen, I wouldn't dream of listening to Richard Strauss's *Four Last Songs*, even though I first heard them at that time – I would listen to *'Let it Be'* or The Incredible String Band.

Stockhausen – Stimmung

I started to listen to a lot of what was called avant-garde music at this time. Part of its appeal for me was that my parents' generation found it totally incomprehensible! Here was an opportunity to rebel, even in the field of classical music.

In 1968, Karlheinz Stockhausen was one of the leading, if not *the* leading composer in the European avant-garde of classical music. He was born in Germany in 1928, and his music has little to do with any kind of Western musical tradition, although he was influenced by his teacher, Oliver Messiaen.

He is particularly well-known for his experiments in electronic music, and it is a mark of how mainstream broadcasting has sidelined experimental classical music that I really can't imagine the works of Stockhausen being played on the radio now. But in 1968, I heard a full live performance of his piece, *Stimmung*, on the radio.

Stimmung was written in 1968, as the result of a commission for a new choral piece. Stockhausen composed a long work for six voices, based on vowel sounds and overtones, and inspired by his journeys to ancient religious sites in Mexico.

Overtones are best described as notes that naturally vibrate with other notes, and that are therefore at the heart of our sense of harmony, or our sense of which sounds 'go together'. If you look inside a piano, and play a single note, you will see that certain other strings vibrate slightly 'in sympathy'. These extra sounds are what gives the instrument its richness, and they are called *overtones*.

When it was broadcast on the radio, I made it into quite an event. We had a big HMV mains radio, which I put on one side of my bed, and a tinny transistor radio, which I put on the other side. This gave me a kind of primitive stereo, with the bass on one side, and the treble on the other.

Then I pulled the curtains of my bedroom, and settled back for 'an experience'. I loved the hypnotic nature of the piece, and the chant-like quality of its repetitions. I don't remember, but I probably lit a joss stick!

Ligeti – Atmospheres for Orchestra

1968 was also the year of the release of the film *2001: A Space Odyssey*, directed by Stanley Kubrick. This remarkable film introduced me to the music of Richard Strauss and Gyorgy Ligeti; Strauss through the opening to his piece, *Also Sprach Zarathustra*, and Ligeti through his *Atmospheres for Orchestra*, which in the film is used for the psychedelic section near the end.

Gyorgy Ligeti was born in Hungary in 1923 and died in 2006. He said that music should not be well behaved, "it should not wear a tie."

In *Atmospheres* the different sections of the orchestra appear to be playing independently of each other, and the rhythms criss-cross so rapidly that there appears to be no rhythm at all. The music floats.

This sort of ethereal music appealed to me as a teenager. It had overtones of mysticism and rebellion. Listening to it marked you out as different.

By the 1970s I was listening to a huge variety of music, and I deliberately set out to hear more. It was an exciting time of musical discovery.

I listened to *Abba* and *Queen* on the radio, I went to dimly-lit and smoky pubs to watch Traditional Jazz bands, I went to classical concerts whenever I could, and I went to, and played in, folk clubs. I went to Gilbert and Sullivan productions, to see contemporary dance and ballet, to rock concerts, and rainy festivals that resembled re-enactments of the Battle of the Somme. There were no taboos, and it was glorious.

I had learnt that all music is worth listening to. There are good examples of all forms, and bad examples of all forms. Good music improves the more you listen to it, and music communicates in musical ways – in other words, it talks about non-verbal experience, to the non-verbal parts of our brains.

No one interpretation of a piece of music is the correct one. Of course, if you are a conductor, or a musician, when you perform a work, it can only be one interpretation. But the next time you do it, it can be – indeed, should be – different. This is true for listeners, as well. People can argue with your judgements (it's rubbish, it's brilliant), but they can't argue with what the music says to you. Your relationship with music is yours. Take Ligeti's *Atmospheres*, for example. It's OK if, when you listen to it, you see flashing psychedelic lights and patterns, like in *2001*; it's also OK if you feel a sense of tension and fear. Whatever you feel is OK, so long as you don't ignore or dismiss it. The composer may have had something in mind, but it's not likely that you will ever find out what it was. Certainly not, if he's dead! So you may as well get on with finding your own meanings, or you will be consigning most music to the dustbin.

Suggestions for Further Listening

- If you liked **Sibelius**, you might like **Nielsen**.
- If you liked **Stockhausen**, you might like **Boulez**.
- If you liked **Ligeti**, you might like **Xenakis**.

Part Two
How Music Has Changed

Chapter Five:
Drums to Symphony
A History of Music

"Music can name the unnameable, and communicate the unknowable"
– Leonard Bernstein

For this Chapter try listening to

- Gregorian chants

- Thomas Tallis, *Spem in Alium*

- Bach, *Brandenburg Concertos, Goldberg Variations*

- Handel's *Water Music*

- Vivaldi's *Four Seasons*

- *Symphonies No. 40 & 41* by Mozart

- *Symphonies No. 1, 3, 5 & 9* by Beethoven

- Brahms, *Symphony No. 1*

- Wagner, Overture to *Tristan und Isolde*

- Bruckner, *Symphony No. 4*

- Tchaikovsky, *Romeo and Juliet Overture, Symphony No. 6*

- Mahler, *Symphony No. 4*

- Debussy, *Prelude a l'Apres-Midi d'un Faun, La Mer*

Some understanding of how Western classical music has developed will help you to get more from it, although you can still enjoy the music without knowing anything at all about it, of course.

I make no claims to encyclopaedic breadth or depth, for I am sure there are huge gaps here. However, this represents my personal understanding and prejudices. Certainly, there will be value judgements – these are my likes and dislikes – they don't have to be yours.

Prehistoric music

Most musicologists, and a lot of musicians, seem to think that music began in the Middle Ages. If this were so, what on earth were people doing for a million years before that?

What they were doing is making music. This early music used

to be called, patronisingly, *primitive music*, but now we know it as *prehistoric music*, and some of it was quite complex and not at all primitive. It almost certainly began with the sounds of the human voice, and the rhythm of percussion, and drew its inspiration from natural and work sounds.

Early music seems to have used a scale based on overtones – primarily, the *pentatonic* mode, so beloved of English and other folk music. *Modes* are scales, generally very ancient, that differ from the do-re-mi scale we often assume to be the only one possible.

They were first named by the Ancient Greeks, who believed that music written in different modes had a different effect on the characters of those who listened. For example, music in the Phrygian Mode would make people strong and brave, whereas music in the Lydian Mode would be dreamy and mysterious. These modes later became the basis for modern scales and keys.

By definition, we have very little evidence of what exactly this music sounded like. It still exists in isolated pockets today, in pre-literate South American tribes and indigenous Australian music.

The earliest flute discovered came from a cave in Slovenia, and is 45,000 years old. The earliest song is Assyrian, and is 4,000 years old, written on clay tablets.

You are unlikely to hear a lot of prehistoric music in your journey in the world of sound. There's not a lot of Assyrian music around. However, you can get hold of some similar stuff in what is now called 'World Music'. I have enjoyed old North American Indian music, Inuit music, Siberian shamanic singing, and Bulgarian choral singing, with its mysterious, other-worldly harmonies.

You can also catch an echo of it in folk music, whether it is Celtic music from Ireland or Scotland, or singing from the South African townships.

Medieval music

Once things start to get written down, we move on to medieval music, or what is often now called 'Early Music', which betrays our ethnocentric and arrogant belief that no one played or sang music until the Christian monks or the minstrels came along.

Throughout the medieval period, folk music continued to be played and sung by ordinary, usually illiterate, people. However, the monks were literate, as were some members of the ruling elite, so their music was the music that got written down and preserved.

Pope Gregory, in the First Millennium A.D., developed a form of religious chant called the *Gregorian Chant*. This is the form of chanting you will probably already associate with monasteries in the Middle Ages. It is sung in Latin, because that was the language of the Church throughout Europe. It was unaccompanied, and consisted of a single, unadorned line of music. This single line style of music is called *monophony*.

The great musical invention of the Middle Ages, however, was polyphony, which involved two or more lines of music performed at the same time. Polyphony was invented and developed in the Middle Ages, but did not reach its finest until the Renaissance.

Songs, like madrigals, and dances were played at Court and in the houses of the aristocracy. We are still saddled with this musical class structure, even now. Polyphonic music has tended to be the preserve of the educated classes, and this music evolved into what we now call *classical music*. Folk music and, much later, Popular music, was monophonic music in the vernacular, and was therefore generally, though not always, looked down on.

The Renaissance in Europe happened, essentially, in the

1500s. It involved a remarkable flowering of Art of the highest quality – names like Michelangelo and Shakespeare, among many others. The word itself means '*re-birth*' and it was built upon the rediscovery of the works of classical Greece and Rome, and the growth of *humanism*, a philosophy that stressed the importance of humanity rather than God.

Here we have the flowering of polyphony, with works like *Spem in Alium*, by the English composer, Thomas Tallis. This is a forty-part motet, which means that the polyphony is made up of fourty separate lines of music, playing simultaneously! And it still makes sense!

Spem in Alium is built like a huge but graceful cathedral. It is a tremendous piece, and it's like going to a banquet and being served duck, and swan, and all the rich things. You can't help thinking that sometimes a nice bit of bread and cheese would go down a treat!

People tend to think of the Renaissance in Italian terms – Florence and Michelangelo, and so on. But it was also a tremendous flowering of English music recognised as such throughout Europe. This is a noteworthy point, because English classical music has not had a very high international profile since the Renaissance. Some people still say that England can't produce great composers, and that somehow it is not in the 'national temperament'.

However, in the Renaissance, English composers were internationally acclaimed. As well as Tallis, major English composers were John Shepherd, William Byrd and Henry Purcell, and, believe it or not, Henry VIII himself, who wrote songs and music for the lute, which was the fashionable instrument of the time. In the world of literature England could also boast figures like John Donne, Christopher Marlowe, and William Shakespeare.

It was a good team for England to put into the European Renaissance Cup. The Final would have been Italy v England. It would probably have gone to penalties.

Baroque music

The music of the seventeenth and eighteenth Centuries is called *Baroque* music. The word 'baroque' is a Portuguese word, meaning, 'a pearl of irregular shape'.

For the listener, baroque music is dominated by the sound of the harpsichord. The harpsichord was called the 'virginal' in England, and the 'clavier' in Germany. It was used for what was called the *basso profundo*, which was a semi-improvised line of music running alongside soloists or the orchestra, giving it a sense of continuity and filling out the harmonies.

The great technical advance in the harpsichord that allowed keyboard instruments to become the dominant instruments in classical music was the invention (or discovery) of *equal temperament*.

Equal temperament is the term given to the division of the octave into a set number of equally spaced pitches, notes, or tones. The number of tones is arbitrary, and in the west it was divided into twelve tones – the seven white notes on the keyboard and the five black ones, all exactly the same musical distance apart. This is not a universal rule; it is just the one we in the West are used to. Arabian music, for example divides the octave into twenty-four tones, rather than twelve.

Bach's massive work for keyboard, *The Well-Tempered Clavier* had nothing to do with a well-behaved harpsichord. It was designed to show off the possibilities and flexibility of the newly discovered equal temperament.

Another musical development during the Baroque period was the invention of the concerto. Secular instrumental music was becoming as important as vocal liturgical music. The latter was still important, of course, and two important works of this nature were Bach's *St Matthew Passion* and Handel's *Messiah*.

The concerto consisted of a work in three movements, about twenty minutes long in total. Essentially, the two outer movements were quick and lively, and the central one was contrastingly slow. The music consisted of a solo instrument, usually a keyboard, oboe, or the recently invented violin, or a small group of soloists, who would be accompanied by, and contrasted with, an orchestra. This is when we get the arrival of the conductor, whose only job in this period would have been to beat time. Often he would do this job while playing the harpsichord part at the same time. If the solo instrument is an oboe it is called an oboe concerto, if the solo instrument is a violin it is a violin concerto, and so on.

There was no such thing as royalties or copyright, and composers earned their living through royal or aristocratic patronage. In effect, composers were paid employees, and their music belonged to their employers. Despite this, their music was carefully copied by hand and distributed throughout Europe, which is why we are familiar with so many of them today.

Baroque composers include Handel, Bach, Vivaldi, Albinoni, and Scarlatti. Major instrumental works that are popular are: Bach's *Brandenburg Concertos* and Vivaldi's group of four violin concertos, known as *The Four Seasons*.

For a listener, the most noticeable feature of baroque music, apart from it probably being a concerto with a harpsichord in the background, is that the melody will be incredibly elaborated. As with baroque architecture, the music just can't resist an opportunity for an extra trill or fiddly bit. Why use a single note, when a trill, or scale, or arpeggio will say the same thing?

You will also notice a few heavily used techniques, also designed to further decorate a tune. The most important of these were *counterpoint* and *fugue*.

Counterpoint is where two or more different tunes are played at the same time, overlapping with, and complementing each other. A good example of this is the slow movement of Bach's *Concerto for Two Violins*, in which the two soloists weave sinuously around and through each other. Counterpoint has been used by composers ever since, to add interest, complexity, or conflict to a melody.

Fugue is a form that will always be associated with Bach's compositions for organ, although, like counterpoint, it was a device used by everybody, and still is. In fugue, a melody, known as the subject, is played alone by one instrument, then part way through, it is repeated by another instrument, and so on. It gives a sense of spiral movement, and there is a delight in listening to the parts chasing one another.

Classical music

Now we come to the Classical period of music. This can be confusing because of the term *Classical music*. To the purist, classical music means music from the Classical period, which was about 1750 to 1810. The main composers of classical music, therefore, would be Haydn, Mozart, and Beethoven.

In 1800 there was no discussion about how to classify music, because all music, whether dance or folk or orchestral, was just music. If there was any distinction, I suppose it was music for the elite and music for the uneducated poor. But now, because communities define themselves through the music they listen to (like house, hip-hop, folk, easy listening, rock, and so on), and because there are more than just two communities (rich and poor) so doing, then we pigeon-hole music into all sorts of genres. Someone decided to call certain types of music, 'classical music', even though the label was already in use.

It is difficult, now, to think of another catch-all term that would do instead. You could call it *orchestral music*, but that would exclude chamber music and opera. You could call it *serious music*, but that suggests all other forms of music are not serious. You could call it *art music*, but surely all music is art. So we will have to stick with *classical music*, if only because most of us know roughly what it means!

Having successfully managed not to clarify the terminology question, we can return to the Classical period. In order to avoid unnecessary confusion, I will use a capital C when referring to music of the Classical period, and a small c when talking about the whole genre.

As is true of the music of all times, Classical music was an expression of the philosophy and beliefs of the period. God was seen as a craftsman, a supremely skilled watchmaker, who had created a universe that operated like a clock. It 'ran like clockwork', in fact. It was mechanical, rational and beautiful. It stuck to the rules.

The supreme branch of scientific knowledge was mathematics, and music aspired to be an expression of mathematics, as did architecture, the so-called art of warfare, politics and the very structure of society. Even social manners and dancing seemed to be manifestations of the quadratic equation!

As a result of this, we can expect the music to be balanced, open to mathematics and reason, and formal. And this is what we find. For all its undoubted beauty and brilliance, the music of Haydn and Mozart is not disturbing, and, where it deals with emotion and conflict, always resolves that conflict neatly, with no ambiguity or doubt.

Beethoven is a little different here, because he was a transitional figure. His early work – essentially, before the *Third Symphony* – was as Classical as the music of his elders, but his later work was revolutionary, and opened the way to completely new expressions of meaning and to the movement known as *Romanticism*. As has often been said, Mozart's music is near perfection and the work of one of Europe's greatest geniuses; but Beethoven, in my opinion, is the greater composer, because he was not satisfied with attempts at perfection, however brilliantly executed. Life for him was not perfect, and the boundaries of musical expression had to be changed in order to express the passion and chaos of life.

There were two major musical inventions during the Classical period that have affected music ever since. The first was the invention of the piano. The piano was a huge improvement on the harpsichord. Mechanically, the harpsichord works by plucking the strings, whereas the piano works by hitting them. The harpsichord is a string instrument, but the piano is a member of the percussion family. Because of the way the sound is produced, the harpsichord's dynamics are limited – the volume can't be changed, and notes are all of the same length and *staccato*. The piano, on the other hand, has a huge variety of *timbre* – the notes can be sustained, sensitive playing affects the tone, and it can be 'hit' quietly or softly – hence its full name, the *pianoforte*.

The second invention was that of the *Symphony*. This is a musical form that totally dominated the following century, and the composition of symphonies came to be regarded as the ultimate achievement of a composer.

The form is generally thought to have been invented by Haydn, who wrote over a hundred of them, and who came to be known as 'Papa Haydn', the Father of the Symphony.

The symphony was an extended work of orchestral music, in

four, or occasionally three, movements. The first movement would be in *sonata allegro* form, the second would be a slow *adagio*, the third would be a *minuet and trio*, and the fourth would be in *sonata rondo* form. As you can see, even though I've already lapsed into music-speak, the form is classically balanced, in that the outer movements are both in sonata form.

What dominates the symphony is *sonata* form. Stated bluntly like this, in purely formal terms, it seems to be a self-imposed straitjacket for a composer, but the artistic skill lay in the ingenuity of a composer's response, just as it does when a poet uses the sonnet form, for example.

A movement in sonata form consists of three sections, known as the *Exposition*, the *Development*, and the *Recapitulation*.

The Exposition is the statement of the musical themes, or melodies (there are usually two of them). The first theme, or *First Subject*, is 'masculine' in nature, confident and extrovert, and written in the *home key*. This means that if the symphony is described as "Symphony Number So-and-So in G major," the home key is the key of G major. *The Second Subject* of the Exposition is 'feminine' in nature (please excuse the stereotyping here – they are the musical terms!), quieter, less 'in your face', to use a modern slang description. This will be written in the *Dominant* or *Sub-Dominant key*.

For those of you who want to know more about keys, please turn to Appendix Two.

That completes the Exposition. Some composers repeat the entire section, some don't. This is then followed by the Development. In many ways, the Development is the key to understanding what makes a symphony tick.

It is here that the composer takes his two subjects, or themes, and 'develops' them by playing with them and by placing them in close proximity, as it were, to see how they get on together.

Because each subject is very different to the other (they will be in different keys and they will be emotionally charged in different ways) they are likely to conflict and set up a struggle.

This struggle is the heart of the symphony. If you want to say what a symphony is 'about', then this is where the meaning lies. As a form, the symphony is 'about' the conflict between two musical ideas. They are musical ideas, not thoughts, but conflicting thoughts, pictures, or feelings may occur to you, in which case, go with it.

Thus, you may feel a symphony is about the struggle between male and female, or the public self and the private self (Tchaikovsky, sometimes), between ecstasy and despair (Mahler, sometimes), between the mass and the individual (Shostakovich, sometimes), between life and death (Messiaen, in *The Turangalila Symphony*), and so on. Whatever the First Subject makes you feel or see, the Second Subject is likely to be its opposite. The Development is the musical equivalent of what Marxists call the 'dialectic' – the struggle, the conflict, the mixing, the compromising. It is a musical argument.

After the Development, in which the original tunes will have been pulled about and played in different keys and by different instruments, they will be put back together in the Recapitulation. In the early days of the symphony, the Recapitulation was exactly that – a repeat of the original themes. However, later composers, who were fascinated by the idea of change and revolution, modified the original themes in order to explore the effect of the Development on the simplicity of the Exposition. In other words, the conflict will have modified the musical ideas into a new synthesis. Our emotions and pictures will have been modified in some way in the cauldron of the Development.

I learned about sonata form from the sleeve notes of a record I had of Mozart's *40th Symphony*. This knowledge gave me a different pleasure – I could spend time identifying the musical subjects of a symphony, and listen to how the inherent conflict between them developed and was resolved. As a result, I always read sleeve notes, even if I don't always understand them, and I would advise you to do the same.

Some sleeve notes are easier to understand than others, but the main obstacle to following them is the amount of technical detail they contain. I found that I picked up the gist, even from these, and eventually – sometimes years later! – it would start to make a kind of sense. So, persevere!

Here is a description of the First Movement of Mozart's *40th Symphony*, to give you some idea of sonata form in action.

The Symphony begins with the Exposition, by playing the First Subject – a jaunty, bright tune on violins, that 200 years later was released as a pop record. In some symphonies, you will find a slow introduction before the First Subject – this was to quieten the audience and tell them the music had started. In this case, however, Mozart plunges straight in.

As was standard practice at the time, the theme is repeated. We then get the second subject. It is a more fluid theme, almost sounding as if it's in a minor key. This subject is closed with an emphatic musical full stop.

This concludes the Exposition. Mozart has set out his stall, as it were – his musical thinking will be based on the different natures of these two themes. So begins the next section – the Development. In this section, the composer plays with the two subjects and mixes them up, to see what they are made of. Later, in the nineteenth century, the Development section became the most important part because nineteenth century composers were using the symphony to express feelings of conflict and struggle – feelings that are particularly part of the development mix – but Classical composers like Mozart still subscribed to the notions of order and balance, so the Development is no more or less important than the other sections – the themes are developed to see what happens musically, rather than as an existential statement of heroism!

After the Development, Mozart returns to the Exposition and repeats it. This is the Recapitulation. In Classical symphonies, this repeat is almost the same as the Exposition, because at the time the symphonic form was seen as a musical form, not a dramatic form as it was seen later, so the rules of musical balance required the pure repeat. As we shall see, however, the nineteenth century saw the sonata form as essentially dramatic, telling a musical story of conflict and struggle between the two themes. This meant that the Recapitulation became a resolution of that conflict, so the repeat had to show that the struggle of the Development had changed the Exposition in some way.

As I said earlier, Beethoven was a revolutionary composer, who needed to break the rules in order to get music to express the passion he saw all around him. He didn't really subscribe to the notion of a mechanically perfect universe. Nor did he subscribe to the notion of a hierarchical and immutable social order.

Although he was German, he supported the French Revolution, and he supported Napoleon at first. He dedicated the *Third Symphony* to Napoleon, only to angrily scratch out the dedication when Napoleon declared himself Emperor.

He was also the first composer to earn a living as a freelance, which made his developing deafness more of a worry.

After the premiere of the *Third Symphony*, Haydn, the respected old man of the Establishment, said, "Before Beethoven, music was about music. Now music is about the composer." Indeed, Beethoven was the first composer to use music as therapy!

He presented himself to the world through his music, in a way that no one had done before. If you listen to the music of Haydn, you don't get a sense of the man behind it. But with Beethoven, you feel you experience his emotions, his anger and frustration, his love affairs, and his appreciation of natural beauty.

Beethoven was introducing the world to a new musical era – the period of *Romanticism* – which was to last for the next 100 years.

Romantic music

The Romantic Movement, which in England in Beethoven's time included such figures as Wordsworth, Shelley, and Keats, grew out of the political and social freedoms expounded by the French Revolution. Romantic artists revelled in a Nature that was wild and uncontrolled, and in emotions that were powerful.

In the case of music, composers used music to explore the world of emotions, rather than of the intellect; to represent mountains and wild places, rather than gardens and great houses. Composers needed greater orchestral power for this, so the brass section was increased, and orchestras grew larger to cope with the demands of the music, such that Mahler used two full choirs plus a large orchestra for his *Eighth Symphony*, known as *The Symphony of a Thousand*. Grand Organs were drafted into the orchestra as in the *Organ Symphony* by Saint-Saens. Tchaikovsky even used onstage military cannons in his *1812 Overture*!

Popular taste today is very fond of nineteenth century, Romantic music. It takes up by far the most time on the radio, so you probably already know some, or, if you don't, it's easy to find some to listen to.

Apart from the piano, which was becoming more powerful as

its engineering became more robust, composers didn't write music for small groups any more. There was very little *chamber music* written in the nineteenth century. Chamber music is written to be performed and heard in rooms, rather than concert halls. It is therefore small in scale and intimate. Concert music, on the other hand, was played in large halls and was a public statement.

The big gesture, the grand statement, was what the Romantic composers were all about. A friend of mine, who is rather scornful of nineteenth century music, describes it as pompous and noisy. It is certainly histrionic, and many of the composers of the time were celebrities. Liszt, who toured Europe playing his own piano compositions, caused ladies in his audiences to faint. It must have been the nearest the Victorians got to a Beatles concert!

Composers, performers and conductors became well known figures, lavishly praised and savagely lampooned. They would have loved it!

The giants of the Romantic period are: Brahms, Wagner, Bruckner, Tchaikovsky, and Mahler. Let's have a brief look at them.

Johannes Brahms (1833 – 1897)

Brahms was in awe of his musical hero, Beethoven – to such an extent, in fact, that when Brahms wrote his *First Symphony* it was immediately dubbed 'Beethoven's Tenth' (Beethoven wrote nine symphonies). Brahms wrote four symphonies, a violin concerto, and two piano concertos. His *orchestration* (combinations of instruments, and the sound-quality of the orchestra) tended to be rather conservative (some unkind people would say 'stodgy'), but his major works are tuneful and contain delightful delicacies.

Richard Wagner (1813 – 1883)

Wagner wrote operas – on a huge scale. His great operatic cycle, called *The Ring*, takes days to watch. If you don't like it, it will seem like months! He wrote other operas as well, notably *Tristan and Isolde*, and they are all long, slow, and densely textured. He wanted to create a new form of total theatre that would overwhelm the audience with music, staging, and powerful emotions. To do this he built his own theatre at Bayreuth, in northern Bavaria, and staged his operas there. Bayreuth still exists to put on the work of Wagner, and it is a place of pilgrimage for his fans. His music is interesting because it uses unusual harmonies, and sometimes he plays a bit fast and loose with tonality. The famous chord at the beginning of the overture to *Tristan and Isolde*, often called The Tristan Chord, marks the beginning of a music that was starting to move away from the certainty of traditional harmonies, and towards an ambiguous style that is not always clear about its home key and which does not always reach a pat resolution. This did not really bear fruit until the twentieth century.

Anton Bruckner (1824 – 1896)

Bruckner was Austrian, and worked as a school teacher and church organist, including being the organist, for a time, at Linz Cathedral. In 1863, he met Wagner, who became Bruckner's musical inspiration. He is mainly known for his nine symphonies. They are huge works, with large orchestras. Structurally, they are like massive cathedrals themselves, building climaxes through long repetition of musical themes. If you like Wagner, you'll probably like Bruckner. His critics complained that the works were too long, and conductors used to cut them mercilessly. Personally, I find them a bit sprawling and heavy, but I do recommend the *Fourth Symphony*, which is subtitled '*The Romantic*'.

Peter Tchaikovsky (1840 – 1893)

If I had to choose one composer to represent Romanticism, it would probably be Tchaikovsky. In my case, his *1812 Overture* was one of the pieces played in Assembly at junior school, and his *Sixth Symphony*, known as the *Pathetique*, was in the first collection of records my dad bought. Many Russians consider him their greatest composer. His music is powerful, and tends to be built like a collage, using contrasting blocks of themes, which conflict and don't resolve. A clear example of this is *Romeo and Juliet*, based on Shakespeare's story, which contrasts the love theme with the violence of the feuding families. The two themes only prove resolvable in death. The same is true with the *Pathetique Symphony*, which is extraordinarily pessimistic. He died nine days after its first performance.

His life fitted the stereotypical vision of the Romantic artist. He was tortured by his homosexuality. He made a disastrous marriage to try to cover it up, and his eventual death in 1893 has been a source of controversy, with the cause ranging from cholera to suicide.

Gustav Mahler (1860 – 1911)

Mahler was Austrian, and, rather like Beethoven was the bridge between Classicism and Romanticism, Mahler was the bridge between Romanticism and what is called Modern music. He is mainly known for his ten symphonies and his songs, although in his time he was probably better known as an internationally renowned conductor. He held major conducting posts in Leipzig, Hamburg, Vienna and New York, and he composed his huge symphonies during his summer holidays. These symphonies were revolutionary, in that, at one and the same time, they are Romanticism writ large and the beginning of a music that would abandon the comfortable certainties of the past, like tonality and 'hummable melodies'. Like many others, I first fell in love with his slow movements, which are languid, beautiful, brilliantly orchestrated, and full of the most exquisite sense of yearning and sadness. It is the slow movement of Mahler's *Fifth Symphony* that is used as the music in the film, *Death in Venice*.

However, because I had learned that I must listen to complete works, not just single movements, I listened to the symphonies all the way through. The other movements can be more difficult to listen to, because he pushes the idea of tonality (writing in keys) to its limit, and even in the slow movements he appears to float in a musical world that has no firm sense of home; and also, of course, the other movements are harder because it is in the outer movements of a symphony that we get the conflict and struggle. The easiest one by which to approach Mahler is the *Fourth Symphony*, which is still my favourite. If you want to hear him at his most melodramatic, then listen to the finale of the *Eighth Symphony, The Symphony of a Thousand*.

Nationalism

As well as Romanticism in the Arts, the nineteenth century was also the century of the Industrial Revolution, the growth of European empires, the rise of America, and the growth of Nationalism.

Nationalism in Europe influenced the classical music of the time. Newly-emergent countries had their own composers, who either tried to develop a new national style or who deliberately used the folk music of their respective countries. Norway had Grieg, Finland had Sibelius, Czechoslovakia had Smetana and Dvorak. Even already-existing countries got in on the act of defining their national identities through music – Russia had Balakirev, England had Elgar, later, Hungary had Bartok.

Claude Debussy (1862 – 1918)

The French, meanwhile, were forging their own musical response to Romanticism, through the music of Claude Debussy. As in the rest of Europe, French composers, such as Hector Berlioz, had fully embraced Romanticism. However, towards the end of the century Monet had introduced the idea of *Impressionism* to the world of painting, and Debussy saw this as the antidote to the excesses of Romanticism – the overkill in the orchestration and the excess of emotion.

Debussy's music was delicately orchestrated, so that each instrument can be heard, in contrast to the overwhelming wall of sound of Mahler or Wagner. The music seems to glitter and shift about, difficult to be certain about, suggesting emotions and pictures rather than telling us what to imagine and feel. All is ambiguity rather than certainty.

Each musical school of thought begins with an attempt to better capture the shifting nature of life, as it is understood by a new generation of composers. This was true of Impressionism. It had also been true of Romanticism. Romantic composers felt that the music of Haydn and Mozart no longer accurately described a world that was dominated by industrial change and revolutionary politics, so they needed to develop a music that embraced change and struggle and heroism, a music based on an emotional response to life rather than the logical intellectualism of the Classical period.

However, the 'new' movement becomes, with time, the new Establishment, and the world moves on, creating the need for yet another musical response from yet another generation. The Impressionists were that new generation. They felt that Romanticism could not capture the elusive and mysterious nature of life. They felt that bombastic Romanticism had no room for doubt and uncertainty.

Some see Impressionism in music as the final destination of Romanticism; others see it as a new form of tonally ambivalent music. Traditionalists must have thought Debussy very strange – he didn't even write a symphony!

His major works are *La Mer, l'Apres-midi d'un Faun*, and many piano pieces. Other Impressionist composers were Ravel, Dukas, and Respighi.

This now brings us to the twentieth century. This is when many listeners start to part company with classical music. You don't need to be frightened of it. It is still trying to communicate non-verbal experience to us, and it is still using the same basic elements of melody, rhythm, harmony, and tone colour – it's just using them differently, that's all.

Suggestions for Further Listening

- If you liked **Gregorian chants**, you might like **Hildegard von Bingen**.
- If you liked **Tallis**, you might like **Byrd**.
- If you liked **Vivaldi**, you might like **Albinoni**.

- If you liked **Bach**, you might like **Scarlatti**.
- If you liked **Mozart**, you might like **Haydn**.
- If you liked **Wagner**, you might like **Brahms**.
- If you liked **Respighi**, you might like **Dukas**.
- If you liked **Mahler**, you might like **Ives**.

Chapter Six:
An Introduction to the
Twentieth Century

"Without music life would be a mistake"
– Friedrich Nietzsche

For this Chapter try listening to

- *Four Last Songs* by Richard Strauss

- *The Rite of Spring* by Stravinsky

- Elgar's *Symphony No. 2*

- *Piano Trio No. 2* by Shostakovich

- *From me Flows What you Call Time,* by Takemitsu

In 1900 the average member of a concert audience would have been familiar with the music of Beethoven, Brahms and Tchaikovsky, if not with Debussy and Mahler. Baroque music was rarely performed, and Renaissance music almost unknown. In other words, there was a consensus of sorts, a general agreement as to the importance of the music of the previous century and a recognition of its great composers.

In 2008, however, the average concert-goer is largely ignorant of twentieth century music, and listeners to popular classical music radio even more so. Beethoven, Mozart, Brahms and Tchaikovsky dominate radio output and concert programming. There was general uproar at the performance, at the last night of the Proms, of Harrison Birtwistle's *Panic* in 1995.

What has happened in the twentieth century to so alienate audiences from modern music? Audiences have always had difficulty with new music. Audiences of the time sometimes found Beethoven incomprehensible, but eventually they grew to accept his genius. Probably, the monk who first sang a different note to everyone else in a Gregorian chant was dismissed by his horrified peers as perverse or tone deaf or both.

However, this antipathy towards modern music has gone on for a long time now. Something must be wrong.

The first music I had difficulty with as a child was Elgar's *Second Symphony*. I remember complaining that there were no 'tunes'! Later, I heard this said about nearly everything modern. What do we mean when we say something has no tune?

I suppose a tune is something we can sing or hum along with, because it is recognisable, and through repetition it soon becomes familiar. Hearing a tune is like meeting a friend. I obviously didn't feel I was meeting any old friends in the Elgar.

The other thing I didn't like about the *Second Symphony* was that it seemed to have no logic, no coherence. The emotional temperature was unpredictable, we would be sailing along nice and gently when suddenly, out of nowhere, everything would get loud and nasty and dissonant. If you're used to the patient build-up of Bruckner, or the plodding emotions of Brahms, the apparent incoherence of much modern music can come as a terrible shock.

I have to admit that, at that time, the Elgar defeated me. I tried to listen to it. After all, I had listened to it in the first place because

I had enjoyed Elgar's *Enigma Variations*. But there was nothing for me to hold on to.

I thought the best way to explore classical music was to follow composers you liked. I still do. Persevere with this approach and you begin to absorb the composer's language, his turn of phrase, his individual sound. But this music is not pop music – a composer doesn't stick with a tried and tested commercial sound. You can go with him on his journey, and experience it with him, but you can't dictate to him where he goes. You need to accept that sometimes he will take another path that interests him, and that is why the music is always life-enhancing and exciting, as well as challenging and difficult.

But I didn't do this with Elgar. I was young, I wanted to stay in the reassuring eternal summer that was Edwardian England, where rivers meandered lazily through meadows full of cows, where cricket was played, and where music still made sense.

Richard Strauss – Four Last Songs

Interestingly, the next piece of 'modern' music I listened to, reluctantly, was Elizabeth Schwarzkopf singing Richard Strauss's *Four Last Songs*. This was another record lent to me by my uncle, who had a big, old, wooden radiogram in his front room, nearly as big as an upright piano.

When he gave the record to me, I thanked him, but I really wasn't looking forward to it. If you remember, he had introduced me to *Tapiola*, which had become my favourite piece of music, so I had to give the Strauss a chance, even though I didn't like classical singing or shaky sopranos.

This was a newly composed piece of music when I was born, and, at the time, was the most recent classical music I had listened to. Up till this, although classical music had spoken directly to me, it was still a historical form. The modern musical form was *The Beatles* and the genre of the pop song. If I liked them, these songs by Strauss might mean that classical music could be 'modern', whatever that meant, and that seemed a bit strange.

Strauss wrote these songs for soprano and orchestra just after the Second World War. He never put them together as a single work, but they were gathered together as *Four Last Songs* soon after his death, and they have been performed as such ever since.

The words of the songs are poems by Herman Hesse, and they deal with the subject of advancing age and death. Given the time when the music was written, I suppose they are also a lament for *Post-Romantic* music, the swan song of a musical era.

I was amazed when I finally plucked up the courage to listen to the record. It was not at all what I was expecting. Post-Romantic composers are not difficult to listen to. The term post-Romantic means the music produced by composers who worked after the Romantic period, but who nevertheless continued to write in a fairly Romantic style. Their music tends to be tonal and lush. Four popular post-Romantics are Elgar, Rachmaninov, Sibelius and Strauss. All four of them remained popular with audiences throughout the century.

Obviously, Strauss would have had no idea that these would be his last songs, and he left no clue as to what order he wanted them sung in, if, indeed, he wanted them sung together at all. His publisher decided on the order, and now it is difficult to imagine them any other way.

The first song is called *Spring*, which is a bit strange for a sequence about death. But you can't have death without life, and spring is the symbol of birth and new life. Death is, I suppose, hard wired into life right from the very beginning. And the music at the beginning shows this ambivalence, with the combination of lively runs – to be expected in a piece about Spring – and a nostalgic rocking between two minor chords. When the voice comes in, there isn't the expected chirpiness – it almost sounds tired, as though this is the view of an old person looking back on youth.

It was that entrance of the voice that made me sit up and listen. I had always thought of classical singing as either Italian Grand Opera, or soloist and piano performing a folk song. In either case, I found the singing style too mannered, too melodramatic. In opera, I found that everything seemed to be sacrificed for power and beauty of tone, and in folk songs the songs lost all their understated directness. The voice in *Four Last Songs*, however, is calm and controlled, rich in its simplicity.

Strauss wrote particularly well for the soprano voice, and it came as no surprise to me to discover that he was married to a soprano. Two other composers who wrote especially brilliantly for soprano were Mozart and Mahler, and it is interesting to note that they, too, were in love with soprano singers. All three composers – Mozart, Mahler, and Strauss – had an intimate knowledge of the possibilities of that particular voice.

The second song is called *September*. It is another poem by Hesse. Strauss was 84 when he wrote this, so images of still, autumn days, must have had a very personal resonance for him. Once again, there is the sense of sadness mixed with a sense of calm and weariness. These songs are not simplistic in their emotional content, and maybe it is this complexity of view that makes them sound so personal and real.

The third song, also a poem by Hesse, is called *On Falling Asleep*. The music here is very tired, but accepting. It contains a beautiful tune played on solo violin, against the background of the orchestra. Solo instruments always seem to personalise the music to me. They bring the big public statement of a symphony orchestra down to an individual instrument, communicating directly person to person.

In 1948 composers were reacting to the horrors of the twentieth century by producing music that was dislocated, violent, and dissonant. This song by Strauss, however, is a voice from the past. It is almost as though Strauss's reaction to the new dissonance of the twentieth century was to compose nostalgic beauty, to use the music to escape. This is one of the main purposes of all music, and one of its main attractions, whether it is an Irish jig, the pop song of the moment, or a Bach fugue. When you think about it, all music is escapist in that sense.

The final song is called *Twilight*, and the poem depicts an elderly couple walking hand-in-hand into the sunset. The final line reads, "Is this, perhaps, death?" The music is slow and sad, but still accepting. The composer seems, in the words of John Keats, "half in love with easeful death" (*Ode to a Nightingale*). And yet, at the very end, the orchestra seems reluctant to finish, to finally say goodbye. Strauss wouldn't have known it was his final music, although he was 84 and facing a major operation. Knowing this makes the final note so poignant.

Stravinsky – The Rite of Spring

My first meeting with new modern music (rather than with post-Romantic nostalgia) was with Stravinsky's *Rite of Spring*. I first encountered it as a child when we went to see Walt Disney's *Fantasia*, where it is the background music to an animation about the extinction of the dinosaurs. I can imagine that some purists would be very scornful about that, but, as far as I'm concerned, there are many possible ways to respond to a piece of music, and if *The Rite of Spring* summons up dinosaurs for you, then that's what it's about!

There is no doubt about it - this is powerful music. It came as a huge shock to the audience at its premiere in 1913, and, when I listen to it even now, it still sounds fresh and exciting. Many people consider it the musical masterpiece of the twentieth century.

It was first written in 1913 as a ballet score, and performed as a ballet, choreographed by the great Russian choreographer, Nijinsky, in Paris. The audience at the ballet were so outraged by the dance that the music was hardly heard in the commotion, but when *The Rite of Spring* was performed as a concert piece the next year, Stravinsky was carried shoulder high from the hall in triumph.

It has become one of the great cultural icons of the century, like Picasso's *Guernica*, or Joyce's *Ulysses*. As a result, people approach it with trepidation, but there's no need to be in awe of it. It is fairly short, especially when compared to the output of nineteenth century composers.

In terms of knowing what it is about, you have a choice. You can either listen to it as a ballet score, or you can listen to it as an independent piece of music.

As a ballet score it tells a story. That story is one of pagan Russian celebration of the coming of Spring, and the ritual sacrifice of a virgin girl. If you want more detail, the story can be found on CD sleeve notes.

When I heard it, however, I had not seen the ballet, and so I just heard the music. Later, when I bought the record, I discovered the date of its composition. Obviously, Stravinsky could not have known of the impending European war that would utterly change everything – landscape, war, art and mankind's view of itself – but we all know about it now, and it is impossible to listen to music of the past without the interference, benevolent or otherwise, of hindsight. So, when I heard *The Rite of Spring*, I heard a twentieth century piece of music telling a twentieth century story.

I don't think anyone would disagree when I say that 1914 was a turning point. It was the end of peace, the end of old political and military certainties, the end of the old Europe, the end of notions of rational progress. It marked the beginning of a century of doubt, re-examination, violence, and increasing alienation. Human beings were forced to confront their dark side.

Freud's new ideas about the subconscious gained credence at this time. This was the opposite view of humanity to the view held by composers of the Classical period. For the rest of the century, mankind was seen as violent and irrational, driven by hidden subconscious desires and needs.

Along came Stravinsky and changed classical music.

Structurally, the music is in two sections. The first one is entitled *The Adoration of the Earth*, and the second one is *The Sacrifice*. The whole piece begins with a Lithuanian folk tune, played by woodwind instruments. Stravinsky, in common with many composers, was interested in folk music, and its use here gives the music an ancient sound, very much like folk music that can still be heard in southern Russia.

The rhythm feels quite flexible here, and it feels like we are in the sound world of melody, but then the first shock comes. A pounding rhythm that never lets up. We are now in the sound world of rhythm.

This rhythm bursts onto the rambling folk tune without warning, just like the horrors of the First World War were unleashed on a nostalgic Edwardian public. Just as the century would never be the same again, so this music is never able to return to the folk melody. It has to stay with the violence and rhythm of the brass instruments and the percussion.

Without the story of the ballet, the title *Adoration of the Earth* sounds very strange. When I heard the music, it sounded more violent than any image I could connect with 'adoration', and the dominant images in my head were of what was done to the earth and woods of Flanders. To me, the title just seemed ironic – is this how we adore the earth?

The end of this section is another shock. There is no traditional resolution, no return to a home key or note. There is no cosy safety here. The music ends in mid-sentence, as it were, abrupt and unfinished. It is as if the violence and dislocation has not finished.

The second section, *The Sacrifice*, is built up of contrasting blocks of sound, quiet with loud. It starts with a quiet, night-time feeling, music that is impressionistic and blurred, almost like the music of Debussy. It is like a quiet night on the Western Front. All is quiet and dark, watchful.

The peace of the night is suddenly destroyed by eleven crashes. It's like the start of a bombardment at dawn, presaging another battle.

Towards the end, Stravinsky writes what is known as a *danse macabre*. I see vast armies of skeletons and wounded and shattered men marching to their deaths. At the end, there is no homecoming, no return to a tonal rest. It is as though the violence and destruction will go on forever. This is no nineteenth century symphony with an upbeat resolution.

The Rite of Spring was a work that ushered in a new musical era to replace Romanticism. Why does this happen? Why did Classical music become Romantic music? Why did Romantic music become Modern music? Why can't things just stay the way we like them, the way we find easy and comforting?

One reason is simply that all things in life have an unpleasant habit of just changing. The main reason, though, is that the outside world – political, economic, social – changes to such an extent that composers feel that they can no longer express themselves and their concerns with the same language.

The certainties of Classical music are fine while you believe that the world is rational and harmonious. Romantic music is fine while you believe that the emotions will lead to noble heroism. But, after the horror of the First World War, and later, after the Holocaust, how could a composer believe any of that?

At these times in history composers try to find a new way of writing music that is appropriate to the new world they find themselves in.

Which brings me to my next piece of twentieth century music . . .

Shostakovich – Piano Trio No.2

It would be impossible to talk about twentieth century classical music without talking about the Soviet composer, Dmitri Shostakovich. He is mainly known for his symphonies, of which he wrote fifteen. This is worthy of note in itself, because composers in the twentieth century were not as interested in the symphonic form as composers had been in the past. Composers no longer felt that the large scale public statement, involving large numbers of musicians performing in large halls to big audiences, could communicate the private doubt and uncertainty that was the modern world-view.

The Soviet system, however, required its musicians to make public statements as part of the artistic face it chose to show the world and its own population. When Stalin ran the Soviet empire, musicians generally did as they were told. The price of not doing so was usually death.

It is hardly surprising, therefore, that Shostakovich learned to express himself in symphonies.

The first of his symphonies I heard was his *First Symphony*. I then heard his *Fifth Symphony*, which is where I would recommend people to start. The *Fifth* is subtitled, *A Soviet artist's reply to just criticism*, for his music had been criticised as counter-revolutionary by Stalin, and his career, family and life were in extreme danger. Stalin denounced him again in 1948, and this time, he would sleep outside his apartment so that his family would not be woken up when the KGB came at night to arrest him.

Shostakovich's public musical statements – his symphonies – were very orthodox, in some ways. The choice was very stark and obvious – if Comrade Stalin liked your music, your music would be performed and praised; if Comrade Stalin didn't like it, you would be dead. This kind of choice focuses the creative mind!

Music in the West was becoming more atonal, more dissonant, which Stalin considered bourgeois and decadent. What he wanted was accessible music that told the story of the glorious history of the Revolution. Generally, he got what he wanted! The music he didn't want was labelled *formalist*, and composers lived in dread of the label.

However, the *Second Piano Trio* is not written for large-scale performance. It is chamber music, which is written to be performed by small groups of musicians, without a conductor, to small audiences, in rooms rather than halls. Because of this, chamber music tends to be more personal, more intense, perhaps more truthful and revealing.

In the *Second Piano Trio* we can expect more openness and honesty, and less worry about the reaction of the authorities. It was written in 1945, immediately after the Second World War, a war that had devastated Russia.

It begins with ghostly harmonics on the cello, a sound that is one of the coldest, bleakest sounds I have heard. This music sounds like a whispered sob, a personal secret whispered by Shostakovich into your ears alone. It tells of cold and loss, solitude and emptiness.

When I first heard it, the piece seemed to me to be about loss. Shostakovich had recently lost his best friend, so the loss is intensely personal; but the loss is also much larger, almost a requiem for the dead of the war and the destruction of Russia.

The second movement appears to launch us into a world of dance, but the harmonies are slightly off-key. This gives the music a feeling of hysteria, a manic sense of living on borrowed time.

The third movement is the slow movement. It is undiluted grief and sadness, beginning with long sustained chords on the piano, which disappear into the empty landscape. The movement is agonising. There is a tinge of Jewish music, which summons up those horrifying newsreel pictures of the death camps in Poland. This Trio is a requiem for Shostakovich's friend, for his country, for the war dead, and now for the victims of the Holocaust.

The fourth and final movement is a dance that is obviously drawn from an east European Jewish tradition. It almost sounds like a Jewish *Klezmer* band. Klezmer music would have been known to Shostakovich, as wandering bands of Jewish secular musicians would have been heard all over eastern Europe before the war. The music was a mixture of Jewish and Gypsy folk music, and a better threnody for the victims of the Holocaust is hard to imagine.

Half way through the movement the music sounds like the dance floor opens up to reveal the horrors of the death camps.

The music becomes nightmarish and frantic, tense and terrifying, until, right at the end, the music returns to the ghostly emptiness of the beginning, to a Russian landscape emptied of its people.

Shostakovich's *Second Piano Trio* is a piece that affected me deeply when I first heard it. That first hearing was on the radio, and I was doing something else at the time, but I had to sit down and wait for the music to finish with me, whereupon I suppose it spat me out a slightly different person. This is what great art does, and why it's worth the time and effort.

This Trio and Strauss's *Four Last Songs* are both personal responses to the Second World War. They are very different – almost from different musical universes, you might say – but they are both intensely felt lamentations that give a real sense of the breadth of twentieth century music.

Takemitsu – From me flows what you call Time

In this brief overview of the century's music, the next major discovery for me was the music of the Japanese composer, Toru Takemitsu, who was born in 1930 and died in 1996.

After the Second World War, Takemitsu worked on American Bases in occupied Japan, and while working there was exposed to Western music of all kinds. He fell in love with American Swing Bands, and also with the delicate music of Debussy. In fact, he was so enthralled that he taught himself to compose Western classical music.

He met the American avant-garde composer and musical guru, John Cage, who encouraged him to treat his Japanese musical traditions with respect and to find a new Japanese approach to classical music, rather than merely copying European and American styles.

The first piece of music by Takemitsu that I heard was a live performance of a work written in 1990 called, *From me flows what you call Time*. I just thought the title was so wonderful, so Japanese. All of his pieces have this kind of title, like the evocative titles of Japanese poems.

I suppose this music is what is loosely, and somewhat unhelpfully, called avant-garde – unhelpful because it may set up a barrier between you and an appreciation of the music.

The title made me curious. It really doesn't matter why you listen to a piece of music, only that you do so with commitment. So what do we make of the title? Apparently, the 'me' of the title refers to Carnegie Hall in America, but that may be a complete irrelevance for a listener (Takemitsu was asked by the Boston Symphony Orchestra to write a piece to celebrate the founding of Carnegie Hall).

One of Takemitsu's private obsessions was the Japanese garden. He wanted his music to be listened to in the same way that you would wander round a garden. You look at this plant, you delight in this view, you stop to smell that flower, you sit down to listen to the gentle sound of flowing water or listen to wind chimes in the tree. This to me gives a much clearer picture of what this title means, and it feels more in keeping with the music. I think the 'me' of the title is Nature, the life force itself.

The beginning of the piece is very like the beginning of Debussy's *Prelude a l'apres-midi d'un faun*, which had been composed a hundred years earlier. The Debussy begins with a simple theme on solo flute, joined by delicate traceries on harp; the Takemitsu opens with a five note theme on solo flute, supported by a *gamelan*-like texture (see below) in the percussion, which sounds very similar to a harp.

The effect is the same in both pieces of music. It creates an atmosphere of fragility and magic, but also a sense of Spring, of the small, seed-like beginnings of things.

Gamelan is a form of music particular to Indonesia. It consists of music played by an orchestra of traditional Indonesian instruments – essentially tuned and non-tuned percussion – such as gongs, bells, xylophones and glockenspiels. It is very complex, and has fascinated Western musicians since the end of the nineteenth century.

Takemitsu's orchestra includes five percussionists. They play an incredible array of instruments, including glockenspiel, vibraphone, steel drums, Thai gongs, Japanese temple bowls, Chinese winter gongs, Turkish drums, tom-toms, rain stick, marimba, suspended cymbals, and wind chimes. This list of instruments represents one of the major changes in classical music in the twentieth century, and that is the assimilation of many forms of non-Western music. This is particularly true in the area of percussion – whether, as here, it is Indonesian gamelan, or, as with the music of Steve Reich, the fascination is with the rhythms of Africa.

From me flows what you call Time roughly divides into three sections. Takemitsu doesn't call them movements, nor does he delineate the sections in any way, but each part has a different character. The first movement, as it were, establishes the garden, the sound of water, and the delicate five-note theme that is the seed with its almost infinite potential.

The second section is, to all intents and purposes, the slow movement. It is quiet and delicate, and makes me think of the Japanese garden on a warm, still night. These images that music produces in my mind are, of course, entirely subjective. Takemitsu doesn't tell me to imagine gardens, and there is no tradition in our culture of direct correspondences between specific musical sounds and particular images. Some sounds lead you in certain directions – a cello sounds warm, or a trumpet sounds military, for example – but music is open to a wide range of possible associations, almost as many as there are listeners. This is particularly true of percussion, because these are sounds that are relatively new to Western classical music.

So, if this music doesn't make you think of gardens, you are no more right or wrong than I am. When I first heard this music, I think it was this very newness and fluidity of interpretation that appealed to me. There was no tradition, so I could respond to it directly, without reference to any outside knowledge.

The third movement begins with a return to the five-note theme of the first movement. This music is not linear – it doesn't move from one place to another, or from one emotion to another. It circles and spirals, and returns to the beginning. It is very much like wandering through a garden. At the end the wind chimes die away into silence, as though the wind has passed through the garden and all is now returning to night.

What Takemitsu seems to be saying about time is that it is largely illusory, and that at the end we return to the beginning.

Conclusion

In this chapter we have looked at four pieces of music from the twentieth century. I have not chosen them for their accessibility, nor for their representative nature or musical/historical importance. I have chosen them because they chart my own, very personal and probably idiosyncratic journey through the music of the century.

Here we have the rhythmic power of *The Rite of Spring*, the post-Romantic sunset of the *Four Last Songs*, the personal response to the Second World War of the *Piano Trio*, and the mingling of East and West of *From me flows what you call Time*. It has been a rich century, and there is much more music to explore, some of which I will examine in the following chapters.

There seems to be a belief that something went wrong with classical music in the twentieth century, that somehow it lost its way and became divorced from its audience. Some music would certainly fit this description (though it can still be rewarding, as we shall see), but there has also been a tremendous outpouring of popular and accessible classical music, and people tend to forget this.

England has produced Elgar, Vaughan Williams, Benjamin Britten and John Tavener; France has produced Debussy and Ravel; Spain has produced Rodrigo; Germany has given us Strauss and Kurt Weill; Finland has Sibelius; Russia has produced Shostakovich, Rachmaninov, and Khatchaturian; Lithuania has Arvo Part; America has Gershwin and Bernstein. There are many I have missed out in this list, but I'm just making the point that not all twentieth century classical music is impossible to listen to.

Suggestions for Further Listening

- If you liked **Strauss**, you might like the songs of **Mahler**.
- If you liked **Stravinsky**, you might like **Bartok**.
- If you liked **Shostakovich**, you might like the music of **Prokofiev**.
- If you liked **Takemitsu**, you might like **Torke**.

Chapter Seven:
Understanding the Jargon

*"Music is well said to be the speech of angels; in fact, nothing among
the utterances allowed to Man is felt to be so divine.
It brings us near to the infinite."*
Thomas Carlyle

For this Chapter try listening to

- *Romeo and Juliet* by Tchaikovsky

- *La Mer* by Debussy

- Any symphony by Mozart or Haydn

- *Fantasia Concertante on a Theme by Corelli* by Michael Tippett

- *Transfigured Night* by Schoenberg

- *Short Ride in a Fast Machine* by John Adams

- *Different Trains* by Steve Reich

This Chapter will be somewhat contentious. It is a quick guide for the general listener, not a textbook for research purposes. The views contained here are entirely personal, and you can disagree as much as you like. Indeed, I would encourage you to do so!

An 'ism' is a system of beliefs, like Judaism, or a theory, like Socialism, or a set of related theories. In the past, in the field of music, these were quite rare. Composers and critics hadn't discovered just how useful isms were in making them sound clever and their music sound important. In fact, in the nineteenth century, composers were so primitive that they managed to write music with only one – a very popular one called *Romanticism*.

Note, by the way, that isms start with Capital Letters, because they are VERY IMPORTANT! This is designed to make anyone who doesn't know the ism feel small and ignorant!

Romanticism

Romanticism has nothing to do with sentimental passion, which would be romanticism with a small r. Having said this, however, people who don't like Romantic music (not the same as romantic music produced by pop groups) often accuse Romantic composers, like Tchaikovsky and Mahler, of sentimentalism, which is another way of saying their music wallows in an 'over the top' emotionalism.

Romantic music was written by Bohemian egoists about themselves or about awesome Forces of Nature. Indeed, Romantic composers often confused these two things! – Awesome Forces of Nature and Themselves! They believed in grand passion, heroic individualism, and the delicious soup of lush music. In many ways they were like nineteenth century pop stars.

Liszt's audiences were full of swooning ladies, and Chopin always got invited to parties. Wagner was famous for his silk dressing gowns, and Brahms was famous for his beard. Romantic composers were the first true celebrities.

The theme from Tchaikovsky's *Romeo and Juliet* is a good example of Romantic music, so try to get a chance to listen to it. This is archetypal Romantic music – it is lush in sound, it is emotional in tone, and the tune is singable. The melodic line approximates in length and quality to the line of a song.

Classicism

Before *Romanticism*, the isms had not really got going at all. The only one of any note was *Classicism*, and that only lasted for about sixty years. The reason for the dearth of isms was the patronage system, which was the way composers were paid in those days. This involved convincing a king or emperor or wealthy aristocrat to employ you. This meant that you didn't have to invent isms to impress music critics or publishers. All you had to do was flatter your patron with music he liked.

Classical music was ordered and rational, written by composers in the pay of kings and emperors, and made to sound like God was in His Heaven and all was right with the world. Not only that, but Heaven was the court or household of the man who paid your salary.

I am being a little extreme and provocative here. This does not devalue the music at all, because music is bigger and better than any emperor, or payment system!

Examples of Classical composers are Haydn and Mozart. Haydn was quite good at not rocking the boat, but Mozart was a bit bolshy and too precocious for his own good.

You can listen to any music by Mozart to get an idea of the Classical idiom. Classical music sounds elegant and controlled. To an extent you can forecast the next note as you are listening to it, because, by and large, it plays by the rules.

The Twentieth Century

Now we come to the twentieth century. By this time the ground was fertile for an absolute epidemic of isms. In fact, they were spreading so quickly no one could keep up. They escaped from the concert halls, and infected recording studios, radio and television, and even pop music. Nowhere and no one was safe.

One of the mutations that made it particularly easy for new isms to become immune to the traditional treatments of scepticism (even that mutated, as you can see!) was the development of the prefix, a virus that originated in the Greek language.

The first prefix to mutate was the 'post' prefix. This could attach itself to any other ism, and so create a whole new musical entity with a new name. The prefix 'post' means 'after', so at the end of the nineteenth century Romanticism could mutate into *Post-Romanticism*.

Post-Romanticism

Post-Romanticism was used to describe twentieth century composers who wished they had been born in the nineteenth century. They still wrote tonal music, which meant they thought music should be enjoyable and audiences should know when it had finished!

Post-Romantic composers included Richard Strauss, Sibelius, Elgar, and Rachmaninov. American composers fit into this category as well, such as Samuel Barber, Howard Hanson and the film composer, Korngold.

Neo-Romanticism

Another particularly virulent prefix was the 'neo' prefix, also originating in Greek. The prefix 'neo' means 'new', so it was able to create the mutation *Neo-Romanticism*. This suggests some kind of return to Romanticism after a bit of a break, but a new and improved version of it. It was obviously an ism created by a marketing executive. Maybe all the letters in neo should be in capitals! 'NEO' sounds much more exciting and modern than 'Post'.

So Neo-Romanticism means 'new Romanticism', but to all intents and purposes it refers to the same kind of music as Post-Romanticism, and often the terms are used interchangeably.

For me, Neo-Romanticism can be defined as music that is broadly tonal, plays with dissonance but ultimately returns to consonance, believes that music should be accessible, is seen by the avant-garde as conservative and reactionary, but still tries to accommodate the musical changes of the twentieth century. Thus I would include as Neo-Romantic composers, the English composers Vaughan Williams, Arnold Bax, William Walton, Benjamin Britten, the early Michael Tippet, Percy Grainger; the American composer Aaron Copland; and the Polish composer Henryk Gorecki.

Impressionism

Not everyone was infected with Romanticism in the nineteenth century. Some composers, particularly French ones, felt that there was something vulgar about all these huge egos (even though some of the biggest, such as Berlioz, were also French), so they tried to create music that was gentle, understated and fluid. This was the hazy musical equivalent of Impressionist painting, and it tried to capture the movement and delicacy and fluidity of life. Romanticism was too bombastic and loud to do this effectively, so a new musical style was needed. This was called *Impressionism*.

Impressionist composers were Claude Debussy, Maurice Ravel, Eric Satie, Frederick Delius, and Ottorino Respighi.

This kind of music concentrates on clarity rather than bombastic power, on the precise definition of a momentary sensation rather than the long working-out of a story in sonata form. As a result, Impressionist composers didn't write symphonies, but preferred short, atmospheric pieces. Images that come to mind when listening to Impressionist music are sea and moving water, and shimmering leaves. Debussy's *La Mer*, for example, is an Impressionistic evocation of the sea. There are very few sudden joins in this music. Everything is hazy and joins are fluid. It is a little like the musical equivalent of watercolour painting.

The use of a harp is a dead giveaway in identifying Impressionism, as these composers seemed to be addicted to it!

Expressionism

Towards the end of the first decade of the century, some composers in Vienna developed a reaction to the ideas of

Impressionism. They felt that life was hard, and that the important developments in life were mechanical and scientific. They were not so much concerned with trying to capture the impressions of the outside world than they were with finding ways to express their inner selves *on* the world.

I found this kind of music really difficult to listen to for years, and I still wouldn't put it on for relaxation.

Arnold Schoenberg, who, as a young man, was a composer in the Post-Romantic style, felt that a new kind of music was needed for this new world. Music as it was could not express the world as he experienced it, so he invented *Expressionism*.

Expressionism is the opposite of Impressionism. The latter was concerned with how the outside world came into us, 'impressed' itself on us; Expressionism was concerned with how our inner subconscious mind 'expressed' itself on the outside world.

The First World War was to blame. After such a horror, people didn't want the outside world to come to them. External reality had become fundamentally untrustworthy. It could, and did, kill millions of people.

The new science of psychology, and the work of Freud in particular, had opened up a new world of exploration and discovery. The inner battleground of the psyche became more interesting than the physical struggles of war. It was almost as though God the Clockmaker had become God the Lunatic! The concept of the Unconscious seemed to define Man as fundamentally irrational, and dark desires seemed more important than logic and intellect.

There are three main Expressionist composers – Schoenberg, Webern, and Berg. Together, they are often known as the *Second Viennese School*, which might lull you into thinking that they wrote pretty waltzes! Don't be fooled – this is not the Vienna of *The Blue Danube*. The composers of the *Second Viennese School* wouldn't write a pretty waltz to save their lives!

The music is completely atonal. There is no sense of key, major or minor, and no sense that one note is somehow more important than another. To achieve this, they use all the twelve notes in an octave, rather than the conventional seven in the tonal tradition, and so no note has the distinction of being the 'home' note. As a result, audiences never know when the music has finished and there is no sense of resolution – everything seems arbitrary. At the end of a live performance there is an uncomfortable pause for three reasons: 1) no one knows when to applaud until the conductor makes it obvious that it's time to clap; 2) everyone in the audience is busy trying to work out what that was all about; and 3) a substantial part of the audience is still waiting for the music to start'

When you first approach an expressionist piece, don't expect the title to give you a clue. Normally, if a piece of music is called a concerto, you can assume it will be about the musical relationship between an individual instrument and an ensemble. In Expressionism, however, it doesn't. I'm not sure why *Concerto* by Webern is called *Concerto*, but that's part of the challenging nature of Expressionism.

Neo-Classicism

After the horror of the First World War, many composers wished to return to a simpler age, one of cleaner, more formal and rational values, and a music that reflected it. They felt they could find this in Classical and Baroque music, which they saw as an antidote to the emotional and non-rational excesses of Romanticism and a worldview that had taken civilisation to the trenches of Flanders.

Although these composers considered themselves to be

Modernists, their music did not totally embrace atonality. They used the harmonic structures of Classicism, but added elements of twentieth century dissonance and orchestral colour.

Many pieces of Baroque music were discovered in libraries and dusty attics at this time, and composers were obviously fascinated by this new wealth of clean, structured music. Many composers began to use Baroque musical quotations and structures, and they wrote for smaller orchestral forces, in an attempt to rediscover the musical simplicity and accessibility of Classicism, but in a twentieth century language.

A wonderful example of this is *Fantasia Concertante on a Theme by Corelli* composed by the English composer, Michael Tippett, in 1953. The title is completely frightening, but in itself reveals the concerns of Neo-Classicism, because it tells us that this music will be an exploration of an original piece by the Italian Baroque composer, Corelli.

1953, the year of this music's composition, was the tercentenary of Corelli's birth, and Tippett was paying tribute to a form of music he considered rational and pure. He even wrote specifically for an orchestra that was based on Baroque principles. Corelli would have divided his orchestra into three sections, and Tippett does the same. There is a small group of soloists, known as the *Concertina*, consisting of two violins and a cello; the rest of the orchestra is another section, known as the *Concerto Grosso*; and there is a third section, known as the *Concerto Terzo*, sometimes known as the *Ground Bass*, consisting of bass strings and a harpsichord. The job of the Ground Bass is to provide depth of harmony and a seamless thread that pulls the music together. It serves the same function as the bass guitar in a rock band.

Following Baroque practice, Tippett decorates the tune with counterpoint, and then proceeds to impose twentieth century harmonies so that the Corelli theme metamorphoses into an eerie modern sound. This is an excellent example of what Neo-Classicism was trying to do.

Audiences were able to engage with the music in a way that they couldn't with Expressionism, or later with Serialism.

Serialism

After a while audiences became quite skilled at recognising tiny non-verbal clues in a conductor that told them when an Expressionist piece was about to end. It is almost as though Schoenberg was worried that his Expressionist music would become too accessible and so he had to make things even more difficult! He invented *Serialism*.

It is still difficult to appreciate Serialist music without degrees in both Music and Mathematics, but essentially it is based on a random series of twelve notes, none of which should be repeated, which is played over and over again in specified orders and patterns. It's a bit like ringing the changes in bell ringing.

As yet, no one has satisfactorily explained to the general public why composers would want to do this, or why they – the public – should be made to listen to it. However, to appreciate this music is not impossible, as I will explain in a later chapter (Chapter 9).

Formalism

The Soviet Union, after the Russian Revolution in 1917, was very keen on isms. It was almost as though they felt they could use them against the West as a form of biological warfare. Thus they unleashed Constructivism, Socialist Realism and Formalism on an unsuspecting public. Composers in the Soviet Union whose music was described as Formalist were usually shot, so most so-called Formalist composers, as you can imagine, lived elsewhere, particularly in America. Stalin's pet-hate Formalists included everybody at some time or another, even Neo-Romantics like Shostakovich. He reserved especial venom for Schoenberg and Bartok, whose music he particularly disliked.

Modernism

Modernism is an irritating ism, because the word suggests that it is to do with modernity, but, in fact, it is only to do with what was considered modern around 1920. That is now a long time ago, and no longer considered particularly modern. This ism will sound more and more strange as the centuries roll by!

The term, Modernist, is used to include all the other isms in use in 1920 that thought they were at the cutting edge of musical progress – Expressionism, Serialism, Experimentalism, and so on. Modernist music tends to be atonal and it rejects traditional forms, like symphonies or concertos. It often uses mechanical and industrial sounds. It is an umbrella term, used to describe the music of the early twentieth century. Thus, Stravinsky is modernist purely by virtue of composing music when he did, and by his rejection of nineteenth century ideas of tonality, orchestration and structure.

Post-Modernism

Prefixes continue to complicate things, and make for endless invention. *Post-Modernism* obviously came after Modernism, but what is it? It's important to try to understand Post-Modernism, if we can, because this is where we are now.

Post-modernism in music came out of the work of avant garde composers, like John Cage, Karlheinz Stockhausen, and Pierre Boulez. All of these had studied under Modernist teachers, but they felt that the 'modern' world had significantly changed – enough to make Modernism an incomplete response to it, or inadequate expression of it.

The changes that these composers sought to assimilate in their music were:

- The development of recorded sound.

- The development of so-called 'popular culture'.

- The exploration of new and exotic, non-European musical traditions.

- The expansion of the media.

- The use of electronic instruments.

Many composers after the Second World War felt that, not only had the modern world let them down by giving them another horrifying war, but that Modernism had become divorced from the reality of most people's lives and had become impossibly elitist.

Their response was to try to abolish the distinction between what was called 'high art' and 'low art' by embracing *Relativism*, a belief that there are no moral or qualitative absolutes, that everything is worthwhile if you think it is.

As a result, Post-Modernism embraces what is called 'cross-over' music, which is music that deliberately straddles musical genres, or that mixes musical traditions. Examples of this eclecticism would be the music of Mike Oldfield or Michael Nyman. It is also a fundamental part of film music, such as the music of John Williams, Ennio Morricone, and John Barry.

Probably the biggest single event in the creation of Post-Modernist music was the invention of magnetic tape. Before then, recordings had been made, of course, but they were recordings of performances made directly onto records that could not be edited. Therefore, recorded music was essentially a copy of a live experience. Magnetic tape meant that performances could be edited and changed. Indeed, music could be created on tape that had never been heard before, and would never exist outside of the recording.

Composers could now create genuinely new music, that no-one, not even the musicians playing it, had ever heard before. The music of Stockhausen is a good example of this.

John Cage

New recording techniques also allowed composers to create music from sounds in the environment, as well as, or instead of sounds made by musical instruments. This form of music was called *Found Music*, and its great exponent was the American avant-garde composer, John Cage. Found music is also known as *Chance Music* or *Alaetoric Music*.

As early as the 1930s, Cage had said in a lecture: "Wherever we are, what we hear is mostly noise. When we ignore it, it disturbs us. When we listen to it, we find it's fascinating. The sound of a truck at 50 mph. Static between the stations. Rain. We want to capture and control these sounds, to use them, not as sound effects, but as musical instruments."

Cage was born in 1912, and became a leading figure in the musical avant-garde, probably more influential through his controversial ideas than through his music, which is rarely played now. He died in 1992.

He described his music as "purposeless play", but also said, "this play is an affirmation of life – not an attempt to bring order out of chaos, nor to suggest improvements in creation, but simply to wake up to the very life we are living, which is so excellent once one gets one's mind and desires out the way and lets it act of its own accord."

His most famous, or infamous, piece of music is called *4'33"*. It was composed in 1952, and is still controversial. Many people think that it throws into question the very meaning of the word 'music'.

Imagine the concert, given by the pianist David Tudor, in 1952:

A concert hall with audience. An empty stage with piano. The pianist comes on, sits at the piano, and opens the lid. The audience waits. The pianist consults a stopwatch, and after thirty seconds he closes the piano lid. After a short pause – for this is the gap between the first and second movements – he opens the lid again, and the audience waits. The second movement is longer, and lasts two minutes and twenty-three seconds, at the end of which the pianist closes the lid again. Another short pause. He opens the lid, and waits for one minute forty seconds. He closes the lid, stands, bows, and leaves the stage to, I hope, rapturous applause.

This sounds ridiculous, I know, when it is written down like this, and I'm sure many in that audience in 1952 would have been equally puzzled. The name of the composer, John Milton Cage, was not completely new, however, so people would have expected the piece to be strange – which probably explains why there wasn't a riot.

Cage composed the piece (I am deliberately not putting the word composed in inverted commas here) after experiencing an anechoic chamber. This is a chamber that is absolutely soundproof. He was expecting to hear total silence, but in fact heard two distinct noises – a high sound that was his nervous system working, and a lower note that was his circulating blood. He realised that complete silence did not exist – even in the most attentive concert hall there would be noises, in the audience members, in the hall, in the environment.

If the audience paid attention to this silence, they would, in fact, hear Found Music – music that would be relative, in the sense that it would be different for each member of the audience – and music that would be different at each performance.

Although many people considered *4'33"* to be incredibly self-indulgent, what Cage was trying to do was to actually remove the organising filter of the composer from musical performance and experience. In *4'33"*, the emphasis is not on the composer, nor on the performer – it is on the audience itself, and each member of that audience will have a uniquely personal experience. What is happening, is that Cage is saying that each person's silence/music is equally important and equally valid.

Now I'm going to ask you to experience John Cage's *4'33"* in the comfort of your own home, or on the train, or wherever you happen to be reading this now.

Set aside five minutes, sit down, and prepare for the concert. I'm going to show you the original score for the work, known as the *Tacet Edition*. 'Tacet' is the musical instruction on sheet music that instructs a musician to remain silent for a whole movement. All you will need for this concert will be the sheet music, which is provided here, and

4'33"
by John Milton Cage
(Tacet Edition)

Movement 1. Tacet 30"

Movement 2. Tacet 2'23"

Movement 3. Tacet 1'40"

a watch with a second hand, which you will provide yourself. At the end of a movement simply relax for a few seconds. Remember not to applaud between movements, as the music has not yet finished, but feel free to do so at the end. It is not advisable to cheer, whistle and stamp your feet if you are listening to this on public transport.

This is not representative of Post-Modernism. By definition, there is no such thing, because Post-Modernism is all about eclecticism, variety and inclusiveness.

To get some idea of it as a musical movement you should also listen to the popular, film music inspired compositions of Karl Jenkins, the electronic music of Xenakis, the repetitive excitement of Joby Talbot, the strange and savage sounds of George Crumb, the complex and new orchestral sounds of James MacMillan, the Japanese and Gamelan traditions of Takemitsu, the electronic atmospheres of Walter Carlos. You can also include Pink Floyd and Soft Machine. There is no end to it, and anything will count, including *A Day in the Life* by The Beatles, or *Good Vibrations* by The Beach Boys!

Minimalism

Minimalism was a mutation of Post-Modernism, first appearing in America in the 1950s and 1960s. Like all forms of Post-Modernism, it was a reaction against what some young composers thought of as the academic and elitist nature of much Modernist music. These composers had been brought up on rock and pop music, and felt that classical music could learn important lessons from this so-called 'low culture'.

The form is called 'Minimal' because composers tried to pare down their compositions to the bare minimum. This was particularly noticeable in the area of rhythm. Rhythm had become very complex in modernist and Neo-Classical music, and Minimalist composers reacted to this by producing rhythms that would seem at home in rock music – almost like an insistent drum beat.

This rhythm tends to be constant and hypnotic, and the melodic themes are similarly short and trance-like. You can hear this in *Short Ride in a Fast Machine* by John Adams. This popular Minimalist piece has the typical hypnotic rhythm of all Minimalist music.

An important technique in Minimalism is that of *phasing*. This word was borrowed from the field of electronics, and denotes the practice of setting off similar rhythmic or melodic patterns at different times, so that they weave around each other and occasionally collide or correspond. This is almost like the Baroque technique of Fugue, but the patterns give the impression of chance meetings and partings. Like in Baroque music, though, the process sounds clear and transparent – maximum effect from minimal technique.

Minimalism has been described as the abandonment of metaphor. This means that the music you hear does not stand for anything other than itself. It doesn't evoke a landscape, or tell a story, or describe an emotion – it is simply musical sounds in time, and "what you hear is what you get", no more, no less.

Steve Reich, born in New York in 1936, is probably the best known of the American Minimalists. He was not a trained musician, but while he was studying Philosophy at college he taught himself to play African drums. In true Post-Minimalist style he brought this African tradition to Western classical music, and created a type of music that sounds deceptively simple, and that is static, in the sense that it explores a moment of sound, rather than a musical development and change such as you encounter with the symphony.

Reich's pieces are usually written for small groups of musicians, like the String Quartet and tape recordings used in *Different Trains,* or the small group of musicians without instruments for *Clapping Music.*

If you like it, it can be hypnotic and trance-like; if you don't, it can be like Chinese water torture!

Other important Minimalist composers are Philip Glass, Michael Nyman, Joby Talbot, and John Adams. The latter has now begun to develop his Minimalism to tell musical stories, particularly through Opera, and so many describe him as a Post-Minimalist.

Some orchestral musicians moan about Minimalism, finding it boring to play, as most of the time they are playing fairly simple patterns over and over again, counting for most of the time.

A Short Ride in a Fast Machine by John Adams is a popular minimalist piece. In many ways, this music is what this chapter has been – a lightning rush through the history of twentieth century classical music.

At least you will now be aware of the incredible number of isms that have affected modern music However, approach these labels with caution – never let an ism affect your judgement or appreciation of a piece of music.

You can enjoy all the music of the twentieth century without having heard of a single ism. I have described them here so that you might understand what they mean when you read or hear about them, but it won't make the slightest difference to the sound of the music. What's more, there are more isms where they came from – Microtonalism and Polystylism, for example – and there will be plenty more invented in the future.

The next century is a mystery, as are all new centuries. One thing is certain, however, and that is that there will be a reaction of some sort to Post-Modernism, and a new musical style will be born. Whatever happens, it will be an adventure.

Suggestions for Further Listening

- If you liked **Tchaikovsky**, you might like **Rachmaninov**.
- If you liked **Mozart**, you might like **Weber.**
- If you liked **Hanson**, you might like **Copland**.
- If you liked **Debussy**, you might like **Ravel.**
- If you liked **Schoenberg**, you might like **Webern**.
- If you liked **Tippett**, you might like **Bax**.
- If you liked **Adams**, you might like **Glass**.
- If you liked **Reich**, you might like **Nyman**.

Part Three
The Listening Experience

Chapter Eight:
The Turangalila Diary
My Achilles Heel

*"In music one should think with the heart
and feel with the brain"*
– George Szell

For this Chapter try listening to

-   Turangalila Symphony by Messiaen – but don't listen to
it before starting to read the chapter.

How do you go about listening to a new piece of relatively
modern music? I'm going to try to examine the process I go
through myself. I come to new music in a similar state to you, but
I realise that I'm already familiar with a lot of the musical
language, and I am fortunate to know some of the background.

One of the so-called masterpieces of the twentieth century is
The Turangalila Symphony by the French composer Messiaen, who,
by the photograph of him I have in front of me, bears a
resemblance to the late Labour Party leader, Michael Foot. I am

giving you exactly the information I had when I first received the recording, and we all have to start with such vague and half-baked notions.

So what happens next?

When I first listened to this music, I was keeping a kind of musical diary; so I can put myself back there, listening for the first time. I shall try to make this process as generally useful as possible. Always remember there are no right answers, only interesting ones.

First Impressions

First of all I just listen to it all the way through, just as I would if I were listening to it in a concert. In fact, I try to replicate some aspects of the live performance, if I can. This means I set time aside to listen to it without any interruptions, I don't do anything else while I listen, and I listen to all of it.

Sometimes this is enough for me to really like it, but sometimes it isn't! My diary entries for the *Turangalila Symphony* record that I fell asleep about ten minutes into the music, and didn't wake up till the end! This suggests I wasn't totally gripped.

Why did this happen?

It could just have been that I was tired. It is, however, far more likely that the musical language was so different from any other I was used to, that there was nothing there for me to anchor on to. It's like when you hear people talking in a language you don't know at all. It just sounds like meaningless jabber, and you wonder how they can distinguish one word from another, let alone how they can make it mean anything! But if you know just a little – a few common words, perhaps – and if you listen to the spoken language quite a lot, you begin to pick up the odd word, to recognise certain intonations, and maybe something of what it is about.

It is just the same with new music. Sometimes it's very similar to what you know already, in which case it's easy to listen to and appreciate. But sometimes it's so different that the brain gives up, and you switch off and do something else or you fall asleep.

This could be called the 'Classical Music is Boring' response.

What did I remember about the music during the ten minutes before I fell asleep? I remembered it being noisy and discordant – what I disparagingly called 'clanky'! It seemed to be atonal, heavy on the brass, and one bit didn't seem to lead easily into the next. I described this as 'incoherent'.

This could be called the 'Classical Music is Rubbish' response.

What are the possible responses to this music after such a first reaction? The simplest one is to call it rubbish, and to dismiss it. This is a bit like describing French as meaningless! Another option is to describe yourself as rubbish – you're not clever enough to understand modern music. Using the same analogy, you wouldn't say you didn't understand French because you weren't clever enough – maybe you were told this at school, but it wasn't cleverness that was the problem, it could have been knowledge, motivation, or practice opportunities – or even poor teaching. All French children learn to understand it very well!

You might decide that understanding modern music is not worth the effort. This seems more reasonable. However, this means that you may enjoy the undoubted delights of beer, but you will never experience those of wine, or the new tastes of a new cuisine.

New music brings new ideas and experiences. Some will be pleasant, and some will be painful; but all will be life enhancing.

The next option is to work at the music a little, to learn a bit about it – which requires no more work than reading the CD or record sleeve notes – and to listen to it a few times to get used to the sound. Sometimes, it is useful to break it down into smaller chunks, just as you would do with a foreign language. At these times I am reminded of the African proverb that says that even to eat an elephant you can only eat one mouthful at a time.

So, having not really heard, let alone enjoyed, the *Turangalila Symphony*, it was time to find out a bit about it.

Olivier Messiaen was born in 1908 in France, and died in 1992. He worked as a church organist in Paris for sixty years, and he also taught at the Conservatoire – his pupils including Boulez, Stockhausen and Xenakis.

The *Turangalila Symphony* was written in 1949. It is a huge work in ten movements, with a big orchestra. It is based on the legend of the doomed lovers, Tristan and Isolde. The title of the music comes from Sanskrit – *turanga* means time, and *lila* means the dance of life and death and love. This information suggested to me that the music probably had religious or spiritual meaning, but I needed to explore further.

Now I knew a little about it – and it certainly was a little – I could return to the music, to consume it in smaller bites and to see if this bit of background might give me some kind of handle on the music. After all, the sleeve notes described the *Turangalila* as his greatest and most popular work, so there had to be something there. Of course, just because the sleeve notes say it is great, you don't have to believe it.

The *Turangalila* subdivides neatly into ten sections, or movements. These ten sections are:

Introduction
Love song 1
Turangalila 1
Love song 2

Joy of the blood of the stars
Garden of the sleep of love
Turangalila 2
Development of love
Turangalila 3
Finale

Just from the titles of the sections alone, now that I knew what 'Turangalila' meant, I could see that this music had to do with love and change and death.

The next thing I did was to listen to the Introduction many times, until I felt it was familiar. In what sense was this music an introduction? An introduction to what? I supposed it was an introduction to either the musical language or to the themes, or both. An introduction to the language would serve to prepare our ears for what is to come, to prepare us for how it is to sound, so that the strangeness of the sound doesn't get in the way of our appreciation. An introduction to the themes would prepare our musical memories for certain sound patterns, or melodic themes, and certain combinations of sounds, or orchestration.

At the time I was coming to terms with the *Turangalila Symphony*, I found it useful to examine new music and my responses to it under the headings of: Melody, Harmony, Tone Colour, and Rhythm (see chapter on the Elements of Music). I still find this useful, because by using these headings it seems more manageable – it's less likely to overwhelm you. But I think it's important to forget these arbitrary sub-divisions when you have finally come to some kind of accommodation with it – after all, music is *supposed* to overwhelm you.

The Introduction strikes me as being in some way about contrasting blocks of sound. There is a heavy, plodding theme, or melody, in the brass, which in itself seems to be made up of opposing sounds – the deep notes of trombone and tuba pitched against the shrill sharpness of the trumpets. This theme reminds me of the walking theme in Moussorgsky's *Pictures at an Exhibition*.

This is one block of sound – the brass section. Another block is the percussion. This seems to trip along, providing a light texture reminiscent of gamelan. Included in the percussion section is a piano, played in a percussive style. Finally, the strings provide a swooping, discordant background.

Messiaen calls for an orchestra of 160 musicians, so the blocks of sound I have indicated here can't be the full story. For example, I haven't mentioned the woodwind here at all, nor the *ondes martenot*, which is an early electronic instrument that makes an appearance in the Introduction, but is more prominently used elsewhere.

The harmonies Messiaen uses are what I call 'close'. If you imagine a piano keyboard, traditional harmonic sounds tend to be based on pitches, or notes, that are some distance apart, such as C and G, or G and D. Messiaen's harmonies, however, seem to be dominated by pitches that are maybe only a tone or semi-tone apart. This almost sounds like the performer's finger has accidentally straddled two adjacent notes! It sounds sharp and discordant. This is a harmonic landscape that needs getting used to.

You can get used to it, though. After several listenings you may stop noticing it as grating on the ear. There is no reason why any particular two notes should not be together, any more or less than any other two notes. It would be strange, however, not to notice that the sound has a different kind of quality to a *perfect fifth* (see below), like CG.

The second movement, or section, called *Love Song 1*, is an unconventional love song. Before I knew it was about the love of Tristan and Isolde, I would have been mystified by this title, because it seems to bear so little resemblance to what we conventionally and romantically call love. The love of Tristan and Isolde, however, is representative of all-consuming love, the passion that almost inevitably leads to tragedy and death – the perfect example, in fact, of 'Turangalila', the dance of life and love and death.

There is gentle music here, often played by the swooping bird sounds of the martenot, but also there is aggressive passion, and intrusions of jazz and Broadway musical. I feel these Gershwin-like intrusions must have been ironic, because Messiaen loathed jazz!

I note from my diary that it was at this point that I obviously got impatient and decided to listen to the whole symphony again. I know the thought process I would have gone through – something like, well I've done the background reading, heard the Introduction, become familiar with the language, and it's only music (a useful thing to remind yourself of occasionally), so what could be the problem?

The Perfect Fifth Made Simple

Of no particular relevance to Messiaen, but maybe of some marginal interest to you, the *perfect fifth* is the simplest harmony found in Gregorian chants. The perfect fifth of a note can be found on a piano keyboard by counting up seven notes (including the black notes), or by singing the first four notes of *Twinkle, Twinkle, Little Star* – the second Twinkle is on the perfect fifth of the first Twinkle!

So, all you have to do to find the perfect fifth of any note is sing *Twinkle Twinkle Little Star*, using your original note to start you off! The pitch of the second Twinkle will be the Fifth (or *Dominant*, as it is sometimes called). If you play the two notes at the same time, you will have created a pleasing harmony.

So I listened to it all again. I fell asleep during the third section! This music was obviously going to be a hard nut to crack. You have to be aware that the nut, when cracked, might not be worth eating, of course.

But I decided to carry on with this process a bit longer. Because of my past experience of classical music, I had learned that it was worth persevering for the pleasure and insight that would come later. Without that work I would not have got beyond Beethoven, and my life would have felt the poorer for it.

The next section is called *Turangalila 1*. Because of its name, I half-expected it to contain some kind of key to the symphony. It seemed to consist of two blocks of sound, repeated. The first block of sound is a long melody on the flute, with quiet quiverings from tuned percussion. The tune is slow and floats through the air, almost motionless, certainly directionless. As we now know, 'turangalila' means the dance of life and death and love and time, so in my romantic soul I thought, on first listening, that this was some sort of dreamy love. Now I know better with Messiaen – indeed, it is best not to assume anything with any music, or you will spend your listening life trying to squeeze expansive and liberating music into your pre-existing experience.

Deep brass and percussion explosively shatter this dreaminess. It comes as a bolt from the blue, and I thought, "Ah, death comes unannounced!" But it became obvious from the clashing percussion and the swooping martenot that this is no static state of death. It was time to change my interpretation! It is really important to be able to do this, if things no longer make sense; but, equally, there is no reason why music has to be logical or conform to some kind of verbal line of argument. Music is quite capable of holding contradictions and non-senses – after all, the very basis of sonata form is the struggle between opposites or contradictions.

But, in this case, if I just swapped my interpretations around it made sense, and a much richer, less stereotypical sense at that. Maybe the floaty flute music was the dance of death – no energy, no direction, no sense of time – and maybe the brass and percussion was the dance of life – bags of energy and noise, rhythmic, messy and unpredictable. Death is the background constant, and it is life, not death, that suddenly comes upon us. At the end of this strange dance, the music suddenly returns to the dance of death, the flute drifting in a void, as the partners drift apart.

I have no way of knowing if my interpretation of this movement is 'right', whatever that means. Messiaen is dead, so I can't ask him. As I said earlier, there are no right or wrong answers, only more or less interesting ones. So go with the one that interests you most.

The next section is called *Love Song 2*. It begins with a strange, restrained dance between piano and woodwind that develops into a light-hearted chase. There is then a series of swelling climaxes in the violins and martenot. Each climax seems to drift off into an echo of the death music from the previous section, before the piano re-asserts itself in a solo passage. Eventually the climaxes die away and we hear the plodding march from the *Introduction* (it's tempting to hear this as the march of time), whereupon the music dies away into the drifting, formless sounds that I have now associated with death.

When you have done this much work on a piece of music – reading about it, listening to it all several times, breaking it up and studying some or all of its constituent parts – there might come a time when you wonder whether it's all worth the effort. I think I've made it clear that it doesn't seem right to me that I should dismiss any music as rubbish, but nor do I believe you should spend your life doing something you don't like and feeling inadequate at the same time. There is just so much wonderful music out there that it would be ludicrous to run out of time in your musical journey because you had spent an inordinate amount of time working on a piece you didn't like.

This is not to say, in any way, that you shouldn't work on a piece of music – it might take you to new and wonderful places you didn't even know existed – but if you have tried to get into China and they won't let you in, go to Mongolia instead! If you want to try modern European music, and you can't get on with Messiaen, try other contemporary composers instead.

But, whatever you do, don't dismiss something you don't like by calling it rubbish. Calling it names won't hurt it! You just don't like it, that's all. Someone else may love it.

So what did I learn from my experience with Messiaen? Primarily, I suppose, it was the simple fact that I didn't like Messiaen's music much – the *Turangalila Symphony*, at least. I don't feel that I am saying this from some kind of prejudice. I have given it a chance to communicate with me. I can even have an informed conversation with someone about it!

However, the process of wrestling with this music has enabled me to dabble in the sound world of Messiaen, and I have some idea, at least, of what I'm missing. The best thing about it is that I can return whenever I want to, because I have not dismissed him as rubbish, or meaningless, or any other of those limiting adjectives that close down experience. Nor have I come to the conclusion that I am useless, stupid or ignorant – adjectives that could have disastrous consequences in terms of listening to new music in the future.

The only conclusion I have come to about the music of Messiaen is that, for me, the time is not right. The jury is still out.

Suggestions for Further Listening

- If you liked **Messiaen**, you might like **Carter**.

Chapter Nine:
The Elements of Music

*"It is cruel, you know, that music should be so beautiful. It has the
beauty of loneliness and of pain; of strength and freedom. The beauty
of disappointment and never-satisfied love. The cruel beauty of
music, and everlasting beauty of monotony."*
– Benjamin Britten

For this Chapter try listening to

- *Concerto for Percussion* by Michael Torke

- Mahler's *Symphony No. 5*

- *Collage on B A C H* by Arvo Part

- *Piano Concerto No. 21* by Mozart

- *Variations for Orchestra* by Webern

The eminent American composer, Aaron Copland (pronounced
Copeland), identified four basic elements of music: Rhythm,

Melody, Harmony, and Tone. Who am I to disagree with Copland? The thing is, he was writing for people who already listened to classical music, and who therefore shared a vocabulary with him. But I would like to suggest my own four elements: Rhythm and Tempo; Form and Genre; Expectation and Frustration; Brightness and Colour.

Rhythm and Tempo

Historically, this element of music probably came first. We have no certain way of knowing this, but it seems to be a reasonable guess.

We are surrounded by rhythm in everyday life – so much so, in fact, that we have largely ceased to notice it.

Musicians distinguish many different rhythms, and this is necessary to accurately play rhythmically complex music, but I don't think it is necessary for listeners. As listeners we only really need to be able to count up to four.

The most basic rhythm, I suppose, is the rhythm of the heart and the rhythm of breathing. These both have the same rhythm, but the tempo of breathing is slower, and the tempo of both is variable. We are aware of the rhythm of night and day, the longer rhythm of the seasons, and the slow one of life and death.

These natural rhythms are in groups of two or four – in and out, day and night, spring, summer, autumn and winter, life and death. It is the most basic rhythm of life – what musicians call 2/4 time, or 4/4 time. It is the left-right rhythm of the march, the work rhythm of the sea shanty, the skipping songs of children. It is the rhythm of most pop music and of nightclub dance music.

Music using this duple or quadruple rhythm can vary a lot in character, from the slow and stately funeral march to the lively Irish jig. The uniting rhythmic feature is the fact that it is reasonably simple to tap your foot to.

The second main building block of musical rhythm, after duple and quadruple time, is triple time, or waltz time. This is a rhythm of three beats in a bar, rather than two or four. It gives a lift and elegance to the music. Instead of making me tap my feet, triple time makes me want to sway and dip.

You can hear it clearly in any waltz by Johann Strauss, like *The Blue Danube*, or in any piano waltz by Chopin. It is not just the name of a dance form, however, but the name that is given to a rhythm grouped in threes. As with duple time, the speed, or tempo, is infinitely variable.

Most music was written in one of these measures until the twentieth century. The rhythmic shock of *The Rite of Spring* in 1913 must have been tremendous. Up till then, audiences could happily tap and waggle away to their hearts' content. But try tapping your foot to *The Rite of Spring*! Even though this piece is completely dominated by the element of rhythm, you just can't tap along with it.

It's the same with the music of Debussy. Debussy combines and crosses rhythms so much in his music that the rhythm becomes blurred and indistinct. This is one of the ways he manages to create such misty landscapes in his music, such Impressionistic vagueness.

As I said earlier, musicians recognise and play many more complex rhythms than duple or triple time. For example, they will talk about music with seven or five in a bar. As a listener, however, all you need is two, three or four: five in a bar will either count as 1 2 3, 1 2; or as 1 2, 1 2 3. Seven in a bar will either be 1 2 3 4, 1 2 3 or 1 2 3, 1 2 3 4. This can be applied to any of the rhythms you'll come across – even Stravinsky. The conductor and avant-garde composer, Pierre Boulez, said that he thought any rhythm beyond 3/4 was 'unnatural'!

What makes it difficult to beat time to *The Rite of Spring* is not that Stravinsky is using strange rhythms, but that he changes them so often, even from bar to bar. This makes it impossible to count it without a score in front of you. The more you try to beat time in this obviously rhythmic music, the more you realise that Stravinsky was using rhythm itself to tear the rhythmic fabric of the music apart.

Is it possible to have music without rhythm? It is certainly possible to have music that is nothing but rhythm, or almost nothing but. A drum solo in a rock band is an example, although you could say that the different units of a drum kit have different tones and pitches and so the music is not just composed of rhythm. (I also know people who would contest the statement that it was music, but let's put this view to one side for the moment.) Steve Reich composed a piece called *Music for Pieces of Wood*, which consists of elaborate cross-rhythms played on wooden, hand-held blocks. However, detractors would point out that each block has a particular sound and pitch. Reich went further than this, though, in his *Clapping Music*. This is similar to *Music for Pieces of Wood*, except that it is performed entirely by handclaps. Its effect on the listener is strange – if you don't like it, it is like Chinese water torture, but I find it hypnotic and restful, almost as though Reich was using pure rhythm so that the mind starts to ignore it and drifts off into some kind of timeless state.

Music has been written that tries to achieve the same sense of suspended time by eliminating rhythm altogether. It is rhythm, after all, that gives us an awareness of time passing. Mahler does this in some of his slow movements, where the beat is so indistinct that, to all intents and purposes, it ceases to exist. But you can still find it – you must be aware of it because you can accurately anticipate the next note or harmonic change.

For musicians, all music does have rhythm, Musicians are counting all the time, otherwise they wouldn't know when to come in or when to stop. Some may not be actually counting but will feel the rhythm physically. But for the listener it is different. You don't need to keep counting or tapping your foot – the music will carry on without you. So some music exists that seems to abolish rhythm for the listener completely. Ligeti's *Atmospheres for Orchestra* does this. If you go to a concert where this is played, shut your eyes, because if you don't the beating of time by the conductor will ruin it for you, although it is essential for the musicians.

Form and Genre

The type of music we believe something is, affects the way we listen to it. This is why I have included Genre as a basic building block of musical appreciation. We listen to a pop song in a different way to the way we listen to a symphony, and if we don't change the way we listen it's not surprising that the music – either the symphony or the pop song – becomes meaningless to us.

Imagine you are an Amazonian Indian who has never heard a pop song. You are probably skilled in the appreciation of drums and flutes, and these musical sounds convey subtle meanings to you that we in the West cannot hope to hear. The scales and modes you use sound perfectly natural to you – so natural they don't need names. At the same time, when you hear a Western pop song, it sounds unnatural, the strange scale seems arbitrary and impossible to remember. In short, you must change your way of listening in order to begin to understand it.

But it goes deeper than that, because the way we listen to music is linked to what we think music is for. The Indian might feel and believe that music is sacred. Maybe it can only be performed by priests, or as part of a religious ceremony. It is never heard at any other time, and is always accompanied by group rituals. Then you see someone listening to a pop song on a radio. (Forget the strangeness of the radio for the purpose of this argument.) How can people listen to music without the presence of a priest? Without a ritual? How can someone listen to music while doing something else?

These concerns and incomprehensions are not inherent in the music itself, but in the form and purpose of it. The purpose of a pop song is not to aid the listener to enter the spirit world, nor is the purpose of sacred music to fill time while driving a car.

Equally, then, the way we listen to a symphony, or a concerto, should not be the same as the way we listen to pop music, because classical music has a different purpose. It is not that it is better, or nobler in some way, or more difficult – it is that it has a different function and so must be approached from a different direction.

So what is the purpose of classical music? First, I will deal with what it is not. It is not something with which to pass the long, boring hours between birth and death, even though this is the way much radio tries to portray it. It is not something to help you relax – a nice cup of tea, or a sleep, will do that. It is not an attempt to capture a moment of emotional intensity, like falling in love, or parting, or even death. It is not a quick photograph or video clip, designed to say all it wants to say in five minutes. It is not a medium on which can be built the peripheral careers of marketing consultants, filmmakers, photographers, fashion designers, or celebrities. This, of course, sometimes happens, but it is nothing to do with the music at all.

Instead, it is a form of communication that explores what it is like to have feelings and emotions (not just to present us with those emotions, but to explore them and see how they change). As well as exploring the big questions, like death and love, it can approach feelings from any direction – but always through the lens of time and change. This time element is why we have to set aside time specifically to listen.

If you find that classical music is difficult or uninteresting, the reason is not that there is something wrong with you, nor indeed that there is something wrong with the music. It may be simply that you are expecting it to do something it was never designed to do.

It will always be rubbish if you expect it to deal with only one thing – event, feeling, state – or if you expect it to be three minutes long, or if you want it to help you feel a particular single emotion, such as relaxed or happy.

It is just the same the other way round. If you are a fan of classical music, it's no good listening to pop music expecting it to explore complex emotions or thoughts, or to be forty-five minutes long, or to deal with religious experience in any detail. Pop songs were never meant to do these things, and you would be missing the whole point.

There are forms within classical music that influence how we listen, as well. You can't listen to a string quartet in the same way that you listen to a symphony, and you don't listen to a symphony as you would a concerto.

When you listen to a quartet, you are listening to a personal communication between you and the composer. It is a private and intimate matter. Just as in a private conversation with a lover, you need to be open, tolerant and receptive. You need, in a way, to give of yourself.

When you listen to a symphony, you are listening to a large-scale public work with lots of other people. It will be about the drama of conflicting musical themes, and the search for a resolution, which may or may not eventually happen. It will be a kind of story – not in words but in sound. When a symphony ends, you may feel as though you have been on some kind of journey, and that you have ended up in a different place, spiritually, emotionally, and musically.

If you listen to a piano concerto, however, you need to be aware that the music is mostly about the piano player. You will be listening for brilliant technique and interpretation. Although there is an orchestra and a conductor, it is the soloist who makes the major decisions about things like interpretation and tempo. So the point of a concerto will be the brilliance of the soloist, and the relationship between the orchestra and soloist – is it a dialogue or a competition, or a conflict, or is the orchestra merely an accompanist?

Expectation and Frustration

There is silence. Out of this silence comes a sound, a note. Unless you have synaesthesia, this note is essentially meaningless. All it can possibly mean is itself. There is now a state of infinite possibility.

Another note follows. It may be the same note; it may be a different one. The possibilities are still enormous. When the third note comes, though, we start to construct patterns. When we construct patterns of sound, we can repeat them and remember them. In other words, we have a tune.

There is nothing magical about a tune. It is simply a group of notes that our brains can remember – not necessarily for long – and repeat.

The simplest way of illustrating this is by thinking of a song. One common form is to take a pattern of notes, then add another brief pattern – call that line one - then repeat it a bit lower – call that line two – repeat it again even lower, and add a bit on the end to get you back to the beginning – call that line three, and you have your first verse. An example of this is Frank Sinatra's *Strangers in the Night*. In the commercial world of pop music, you need to establish that tune and make it memorable as soon as possible.

This repetition is not the preserve of the popular song. The beginning of Beethoven's *Fifth Symphony* and the beginning of Mendelssohn's *Fingal's Cave* use something similar.

When a tune, or melody, or theme (all words for the same thing) is played, there is a note on which it feels finished, at rest. We anticipate this note and feel satisfied when it is reached. It is like a full stop.

In the twentieth century, serialist composers tried to break down this tyranny of the home note by using a twelve-note scale, in which all the notes have equal value and importance, and there is no sense of a natural home. This made tunes sound frustratingly random and incomplete.

This is not to say that music should not sound random and incomplete. As long as life contains randomness and incompletion, so should music. We just need to be aware of these things.

Expectation and frustration play a crucial role in harmony and orchestration, as well. The appreciation of harmony depends on our ability to hear more than one note simultaneously. If we hear a C and a G played together, the combined sound seems to be natural, they seem to 'go together', they don't fight with each other. If we add an E the chord sounds richer, but the new note seems to fit perfectly. This is called a C major *triad*. These notes we expect to go together, and it sounds pleasing and reassuring when they do.

There are lots of examples of such chords, in all the different keys, and, although they are all different in emotional feel, they all sound right and pleasing to the ear. This constitutes tonal music. All pop music, and most classical music before the twentieth century is tonal.

However, if you play a C major triad, and now add an F# (sharp), for example, there will be a sense that the new note is 'wrong' and it stands out from the others. C and F# don't 'go together', they clash, and it 'sounds horrible'. In effect, it has frustrated our desire for the restful chord. This is the realm of *atonality*, and is the basis of much twentieth century classical music. Once you start putting notes together that shouldn't be together, there's no telling where it might end! This helps to explain why so much modern music sounds restless, frustrating, and violent. It is a function of dissonance.

If you don't know the names of chords and musical notes, it doesn't matter. Almost nobody can give a name to a note when they hear it. To be able to do so is called having *perfect pitch*, and it is very very rare. Mozart had it, but he was a one-off! When I say C and G go together and F# doesn't fit in with them, you just need to be aware that certain combinations of notes sound right, and some don't.

Composers, of course, deliberately exploit this desire the listener has for completion and resolution. Even in a period when such harmony was assumed and universal, composers like Mozart would slip in a little dissonance to take us by surprise. Even the occasional note that is outside the expected key or scale – known as an *accidental*, for some obscure reason – will make us sit up and pay attention. A good example of this is the piano tune in the slow movement of Mozart's *Piano Concerto No.21*, which was used in the film *Elvira Madigan*.

This contains an accidental, which is the note that sounds

slightly alien and which the tune seems to lean on. Some performers exaggerate this note – a practice that distorts the simplicity of the music.

Equally, modern composers will reverse this, and insert a conventional harmony in an otherwise dissonant piece. James MacMillan does this in *The Confession of Isobel Gowdie*, and so does the Estonian composer, Arvo Part, in his *Collage on B A C H.*

This movement between the expected and the unexpected, between the reassuring and the shocking, is what makes classical music fluid and emotionally complex. Just as in life, we are not allowed to drift off into a non-changing fantasy world of everlasting harmony and perfectly predictable combinations. That is the world of so-called *ambient* music.

Brightness and Colour

Musicians talk about the 'brightness' of a sound, or the 'colour' of a sound, or the 'warmth' of a sound. What do they mean?

It's a way of talking about the quality of a sound in words. By definition, it is vague and ambiguous, and full of contradictions, but it's the best we can do. If words could express the quality of sound precisely, we'd have no need of music.

Each instrument in an orchestra has a different sound, obviously. A piccolo has a very different feel to a cello. We could call that different quality a difference in tone colour. Or you might say the cello has a warmer sound than a piccolo.

Generally speaking, lower pitched instruments – cello, double bass, bassoon, oboe, tuba, French horn – are described as warmer and darker. The higher instruments – piccolo, flute, trumpet, sometimes violins – are described as cool, light, thin.

When a composer mixes different instruments, he can get

different tone colours, and these colours significantly affect the meaning of the music. For example, if we hear a piccolo, it may sound cold and shrill, but add a flute, which is a similar sound in many ways, and the combined sound gets richer and warmer. Add a bassoon and you have an element of darkness in the mix.

It is like mixing paint.

Some composers have a reputation for being particularly skilful at mixing orchestral colours. These include Mendelssohn, Debussy and Richard Strauss. When you listen to these composers, it is worth paying special attention to the way they combine instruments to achieve subtle variations in sound quality. But all composers have their own sound colour, which is what makes their music recognisably theirs. This recognition of a particular composer's style and colour, for the listener, is something that comes with experience. And then you will be able to hear subtle influences and similarities between composers.

For me, it is one of the little miracles of composition. In the past, composers had no way to test out new combinations. How on earth did they know what the effect would be when they added an oboe? I know there is a certain amount of teachable knowledge in orchestration, and probably most of it is bread and butter stuff for composers. These days, a lot of them earn most of their money through orchestrating film scores. But I like to think that these little magical combinations – most of which are so subtle that I can't tell what has happened, or what instruments are being used – are little sparks of genius.

Careful attention to tone colour is how to get through serialist music. A composer like Webern has a fearsome reputation. Even classical music enthusiasts avoid him like the plague, saying he's too difficult, there's nothing to hold on to. It's true – his music is hard to listen to in the normal way.

Webern was fascinated by the tiny things of life. The story is told of him walking in the Alps with a friend. His friend stopped to admire the breathtaking view of mountains and glaciers and valleys. "How beautiful it is!" he exclaimed. Webern bent down to study a pebble. "Yes, it is," he agreed.

You need to approach his music like this. Fortunately, his pieces are not very long, because they require intense concentration. You need to take them note by note, listening carefully for each individual colour and the subtle combinations of notes that are rarely expected to be together.

It is hopeless if you look at the whole thing. It will seem disjointed and ugly. Listen to the tiny details of colour second by second – look at the pebbles that make up the beach, not at the whole beach.

This approach requires you to hold several notes, or sounds, in your mind at once, but all music requires you to do this.

Orchestration is a very complex skill, and you never stop finding new delights. Any composer reading this will probably be horrified – all those years of study boiled down to a few simplistic sentences!

But this book is not for composers; it is for listeners who need a light at the end of the tunnel, and who need to feel there is some hope for them in the apparently hostile world of classical music.

I'll try to formulate the approach in a bullet-point format for easy reference:

- Be aware of the type of music it is – what period (Classical, Romantic, etc.), and form (Symphony, Concerto, etc.), and listen appropriately.

- Be aware of how the music gets you to anticipate what's

going to happen, and how sometimes it frustrates those expectations, and sometimes it fulfils them.

- Monitor the images and feelings that come into your mind as you listen, including the uncomfortable ones. Notice how they change.

- Listen carefully to the details of colour and orchestration. Try to identify the different instruments being used (not always easy!).

- Listen to the whole piece, more than once. Don't use it as background; in fact, don't use it at all – allow it to use you!

- Occasionally, follow a particular instrument through the music. It doesn't matter which one, or ones. This will reveal new music, even in the most familiar piece, and will help to develop aural concentration.

Recommended Further Listening

- If you liked **Torke**, you might like **Aho**.
- If you liked **Mahler**, you might like **Dvorak**.
- If you liked **Mozart**, you might like **Gluck**.
- If you liked **Part**, you might like **Gorecki**.
- If you liked **Webern**, you might like **Berg**.

Chapter Ten:
Living Composers

*"A good composer is slowly discovered; a bad composer
is slowly found out."* Ernest Newman

For this Chapter try listening to

- *The Chairman Dances* by John Adams

- *On the Transmigration of Souls* by John Adams

- *The Beserking* by James Macmillan

- *Black Angels* by George Crumb

- *Symphony No. 4* by Hans Werner Henze

As a general rule, living composers of classical music don't really get
a good press. People tend to dismiss it as 'noise', or 'rubbish', or 'not
music'. Obviously, statements like this don't make it easy to listen
to. The baggage you are bringing to the music is debilitating.

So, how do you go about listening to brand new music?

In some ways, it's easier, because no one can tell you what to feel or think. When you listen to a Beethoven symphony, for example, you are in the presence of 200 years of performance and interpretation. To an extent, people's minds are already made up. Because Beethoven is famous, you might feel nervous about responding openly to his music. If you don't like it, you can feel inadequate; if you do like it, maybe it's just because you've been told it's good.

However, with genuinely new music, no one really knows what to think. Some critics and musicologists will pretend that they do, but they are guessing really.

Greatness in a composer is a matter partly of time. At the moment of composition, new music is communicating to us in a new language. We are bound to find it challenging. Each composer speaks to us in his or her own language, made out of the same notes but with a unique intonation and vocabulary. Each note is a syllable, each bar is a word, each pattern or tune is a sentence.

This is why new music is a puzzle. The first performance of Beethoven's *Fifth* was greeted by incomprehension, Tchaikovsky's *Piano Concerto* was dismissed as derivative, there was a riot at the first performance of *The Rite of Spring*. There is nothing new about finding contemporary music difficult!

In this chapter, I will talk about some contemporary composers. They are examples of the variety of music being written around the turn of the twenty-first century. They are not totally representative, nor have they been chosen because they are recognised as great. I have chosen them because I like them, and you might like them too.

John Adams

John Adams was born in 1947, in Worcester, Massachusetts, USA. He is probably the most successful of modern American composers, with a large body of work performed regularly at home and abroad.

He studied music at Harvard, and then moved to San Francisco. This is interesting in itself, because his music comes out of two musical traditions – the academic music of the East Coast, and the more populist ideas of minimalism.

I first encountered his music in the 1990s, when I saw him conduct the Halle Orchestra in Manchester in a performance of his piece called, *The Chairman Dances*. This is a concert piece linked to his opera, *Nixon in China,* about the 1972 American peace initiative with communist China.

At that time he was known as a Minimalist composer, mostly known in Europe for his short, exciting *Short Ride in a Fast Machine*. This exhibits all the marks of minimalist music – a driving rhythm, repeated musical phrases, phasing, in which lines of repeated music are set off at different times so that their rhythms and cadences clash and coincide at apparently random times. There is no symphonic development, and at the end we are in the same place as at the beginning. It is, in fact, just like an exciting ride on a fairground machine, in that after all the screams we end up at the sudden peace of the beginning.

The very fact that Adams writes operas seems to undermine his pure minimalist credentials, because minimalism tends to reject the notion that music can, or should, mean anything other than the music itself.

Opera, by its very nature, tells stories that go outside the music. Not only does Adams tell dramatic stories, but also the subjects of his operas are controversial and taken from the modern political world.

Nixon in China is about President Nixon's peace initiative with China; his next opera, *The Death of Klinghoffer,* was about the Israeli–Palestinian conflict and its attendant terrorism; in 2005, his opera, *Doctor Atomic,* about Robert Oppenheimer and the development of the atomic bomb, received its premiere.

This mix of musical approaches has proved to be very fertile for Adams. His minimalism encourages him to use strong rhythms and exciting orchestration. His operatic writing has produced an interest in writing for voice, and in allowing music to directly comment on the big issues of our time.

Combined with all this is an accessible style that makes Adams a good living composer for nervous listeners to start with.

Any work by Adams is worth listening to, but I'm going to talk about one of his recent pieces, *On the Transmigration of Souls*, which was commissioned from him by the New York Philharmonic Orchestra, to mark the terrorist attacks on the World Trade Centre on 11 September 2001.

On the Transmigration of Souls is performed by a large orchestra, a child choir and an adult choir, and a pre-recorded tape for the text, which is made up of words and extracts from the 'Missing' posters that families put up around the destroyed buildings, in a desperate attempt to trace missing relatives.

Is this great music?

It is impossible to say, one way or the other, with music that is so close to us in time. Added to this, the difficulty in assessing the quality of music is made more difficult by the very diversity of post-modern music. Who knows what will survive and what will sink without trace?

They are the wrong questions to ask.

More useful are questions like; does the music make me feel anything? Or, does it spark off interesting pictures, or colours, or thoughts?

I feel *On the Transmigration of Souls* touches very powerful emotions, and summons up powerful images.

The piece begins with recorded sounds of the city – traffic and footsteps, snatches of conversation. It is as though the city has been invited into the concert hall, to dislodge us from our comfy seats, and to share in a public event.

Out of the sounds of the city and its sirens comes the voice of a boy, with the repeated word, 'Missing.' It would have been the obvious thing for Adams to do, reading the names of the dead, but to base the text on those never found brings it right into the present – these people are, after all, still missing.

In fact, Adams avoids the obvious quite deliberately. He has said that he doesn't want the piece called a Requiem, because it does not share the necessary liturgical assumptions. Instead, he calls it a 'memory space', to which people can go to be alone with their thoughts and emotions. He compares it to a huge cathedral, where an individual feels in personal communion with souls that have changed utterly, or transmigrated.

However, the transmigration of souls in the title does not just apply to the dead. Adams insists that this music is built around those who were left behind. The text is made up of their words, and he insists that their souls, too, have changed as a result of the events of 9/11.

This is more than the sentimental music of the moment, and why it can touch all of us. In a sense, as a result of such slaughter, all our souls have transmigrated.

When the choir enters, it does so in the high registers, giving the sound an ethereal, ghostly feel, reminiscent of parts of *The Planets*, by Holst. The sound is cold. This cold emptiness with the litany of names is the grief of those left behind in a vacancy of incomprehension.

Adams's text is not poetical or highly charged. He noticed that in times of personal catastrophe, people don't fly to poetry, but to simple, direct language – "I am waiting". "She had the voice of an angel", "You will never be forgotten".

As a result of this unaffected language, we feel the reality of these people. These are real families that have been shattered.

Round about eleven minutes into the work we get the first hint of brass and percussion. Adams did not want to describe the events of 9/11 – it would be unnecessary after all the media coverage, as well as slightly voyeuristic – so the predominant mood of the music is quiet, sad, and reflective. It is eleven minutes before the orchestra begins to flex its considerable muscle, in waves of sound that are almost like sobs of uncontrollable grief.

The next climax is about sixteen minutes in, with a huge burst of panic on the line "I wanted to dig him out. I know just where he is." I see images of people running down the street ahead of the dust cloud, while behind it all, the towers are crumbling and falling. The use of the brass, particularly the trombones, is like Sibelius's use of them in his seventh Symphony – huge, powerful, almost majestic.

The music then returns to the litany of names, and eventually back to the quiet street noises of the beginning.

This sort of music, in the jargon, is known as *Occasional Music* – in other words, music that was composed for a particular event, or occasion. Few of these pieces survive for very long after the occasion, which is why some critics dismiss them as unimportant music. Certainly, it is true that this music is unlikely to be listened to often – it is far too harrowing for that – but it fulfils an important function, both as a memorial and 'memory space', and also as a ritual of connection, a reminder of our common humanity. In a way, this is what all music does.

We are unable to deny the power of this music. As to its 'greatness', we shall just have to wait and see.

James Macmillan

James Macmillan was born in Ayrshire, Scotland, in 1959, and he is seen by many as the leading British composer of his generation. His concerto for piano and orchestra was composed when he was thirty, and has the intriguing title, *The Berserking*.

With such a title you can't help but feel the meaning of the music somehow lies in the meaning of the title. But, as I'm saying over and over again, you don't need to get sucked into this belief that a piece of music has to mean a particular thing.

However, the title is there and asking to be looked up in the dictionary. Here it is:

Berserk – wild Norse warrior fighting with mad frenzy
(Oxford Concise Dictionary)

Originally, 'to go berserk' applied to the state of rage and blood lust that Highland fighters would need to work up to turn them into ferocious and fearless warriors, often through the use of alcohol.

The first bars sound unusual. The sound is made by all the brass and woodwind players in the orchestra opening and closing their valves and keys, without blowing into the instruments at all. They are then joined by the string players hitting their instruments until the percussion heralds the brass and piano.

What does this mean?

Again, it is the wrong question to ask, just as is the question about greatness and whether the music will 'last'.

It is a kind of magic, in that what matters is what it summons up for you. Of course, now that you know that berserking is the process of working yourself up into a fighting rage, you might be imagining some kind of savage dance. But equally, you might see a railway train, or a fire, or you might see a dark screen explode into different colours. These are all pictures I have had listening to this music, and there are thousands more.

Macmillan is an ardent fan of Glasgow Celtic Football Club, and he has compared the repetitive rhythm to a football chant; excited, tribal and taunting.

In fact, the initial impulse to write this came to Macmillan while watching Celtic play Partisan Belgrade. His home team fought hard, with spirit and wild determination, but lost. He felt that this was somehow a comment on the Scottish character.

Whatever pictures or feelings you get, however, they are probably not gentle and peaceful. This music is percussive and hard. The main theme in the piano is repetitive and rhythmic.

The whole of this movement seems to represent that energy that makes lots of noise but gets nowhere, and that reaches no conclusion. From this display of aggressive masculinity comes the feminine slow movement.

Macmillan bases this movement on a *modal scale* that builds slowly on the piano, note by note. This is gentle and floating, almost improvisatory.

In the middle of this slow movement the modal nature of the music takes on the ancient sound of traditional Hebridean singing, in which voices enter with the same basic tune but in a staggered fashion – a kind of floating musical 'follow the leader' called *heterophony*. The effect is almost like keening voices in the mist. It is the opposite energy to that of the first movement.

The third and final movement returns us to the world of male berserking. It is now clear that we are in the structural world of the Classical or Romantic concerto, with two energetic movements either side of an introspective slow movement.

After a wild cacophony, the music breaks into a section of minimalist repetition. To me, this sounds like breaking out of a noisy factory into reassuring sunshine and wind.

Three times we get this minimalist section, or something like it, and three times it disintegrates into discordant bangs. All this climaxes in a return of the first movement theme, then virtuoso crashes on the side drum.

But this is not the final statement, and not what we take away with us from the music. Macmillan gives us a *coda*.

A coda is a section appended to a piece of music to act as an extended full stop. It is Italian for 'tail'.

The simplest way of finishing a piece of music is with a single massive chord, usually the home chord. Sometimes, however, such an ending would be too sudden and would make the listener feel out of balance, as though hitting a wall while running.

If a composer writes a coda, this gives time for the musical energy to come to a halt, and allows the listener to take breath and perhaps reflect on the experience. Rock music uses the *outro*, pop songs use *fadeouts*, and these are forms of coda. Beethoven, in particular, turned the coda into an art form in itself.

The coda of *The Berserking* is a complete contrast to what came before. It consists of piano and celeste gently and continuously playing. It is the Celtic land of soft mist and shimmering water, rather than warlike football terraces. This is the peace we are left with at the end.

George Crumb

The American composer, George Crumb, was born in West Virginia in 1929. He spent 30 years teaching music at the University of Pennsylvania.

His music tends to be composed for small ensembles, often of amplified instruments. In this way his music is typically post-modern. It has also been described, interestingly, as 'fragile'. This fragility comes from his use of small instrumental forces – the quartet, for example, is intimate in scale and, relative to an orchestra, delicate in sound.

His quartet for electric strings, *Black Angels*, subtitled *Thirteen Images from the Dark Land*, written in 1970, was inspired by the Vietnam War. The image of the Black Angel is traditionally the image of the Devil, though, for me, the Vietnam War has superimposed pictures of helicopter gunships.

In 1990, George Crumb said of that time, "Things were turned upside down. There were terrifying things in the air … they found their way into Black Angels."

The quartet is in three movements, entitled *Departure*, *Absence*, and *Return*. Each movement is made up of a number of sections, or images, that make up the thirteen images of the subtitle. The names of these images are:

I Departure
    1 Threnody I: Night of the Electric Insects
    2 Sound of Bones and Flutes
    3 Lost Bells
    4 Devil-music
    5 Danse Macabre

II Absence
    6 Pavana Lachrymae
    7 Threnody II: Black Angels!
    8 Sarabanda da la Muerte Oscura
    9 Lost Bells (Echo)

III Return
    10 God-music
    11 Ancient Voices
    12 Ancient Voices (Echo)
    13 Threnody III: Night of the Electric Insects

From these structural titles, the thirteen images, we get an impression that this music will not be peaceful or happy.

Supposedly, on one level, Crumb says the music represents the journey of a soul. Departure is the soul's fall from Grace, or departure from God; Absence represents the soul's annihilation, or absence from God; and Return is the soul's Redemption, or return to God.

The quartet opens with the first *threnody*. A threnody is a song of lamentation. It opens suddenly and frantically. It sounds like the hysteria of falling grief. This is the fear of the falling soul, but it is also the buzz of flies on the battlefield and the hovering helicopters in Vietnam.

I found this music shocking when I first heard it. To an extent, it doesn't sound like anything we normally call 'music'. Sit down, and listen to it like you would read a book. It is a book that will shock and disturb you, because it is about war and violence, about the descent of the soul into evil, death and annihilation. The music will not be – cannot be – pretty, tuneful, or harmonious.

This first image lasts for one minute twenty seconds, only to run into the second image of bones and flutes. These sounds are still played by members of the quartet, and involve strange mouth sounds and water-tuned crystal glasses.

The third image is quiet and distant, like a tropical night and a memory of death. It is characterised by quiet wailing sounds, as though the soul is crying as it falls from Grace, a feeling of abandonment.

The Devil-music is a grotesque screeching with outbursts of percussion. To me it is a mix of horrific taunting and pain, the strings of the instruments creaking and stretching. It is as though the Devil is laughing at the lost soul – I can't help feeling that if the Devil could laugh this is what it would sound like!

An eerie *Danse Macabre* brings the movement to a close, with the players hitting their instruments to provide the dance beat. It is jerky and distorted. The soul has fallen in pain and anguish, only to be mocked by the forces of evil.

The second movement, *Absence*, begins with an elegant dance of tears, with the sound reminiscent of church music, but with eerie squeaks on the violin. The image I have is of a lost soul, floating in a kind of cathedral space. Sometimes, I see a surreal jungle with watching, paranoid eyes.

The second *threnody*, which follows, contains violent shouts and the return of the buzzing flies. Now, it feels to me that the Black Angels of the title represent the Devil, the helicopters of war, and the swarms of flies on rotten carcasses.

After the *threnody*, we get another slow and stately dance, with echoes of the opening of the movement. It seems that the structure is balanced in some way, with the second half acting as a mirror to the first half.

The third movement charts the return to a moral universe. It begins with *God-music*, which is peaceful but distant. It contrasts with the energetic but discordant *Devil-music*. It is eerily beautiful, a memory of tenderness that reawakens the soul.

There are then two short images, called *Ancient Voices*, played *pizzicato* (which means the strings are plucked and sharp, rather than bowed), sounding like dripping water in caves. These images, too, are like distant, distorted memories.

The movement ends with the final *threnody*, which contains echoes of all the previous images. It is called, like the first image, *Night of the Electric Insects*, and it sounds dry and scurrying. We are, indeed, back at the beginning, with no sense of final resolution. We seem condemned to endlessly repeat the Fall from Grace, through Original Sin, or through violence and brutality.

Like *On the Transmigration of Souls*, this music was inspired by a huge public event – Adams by the terrorist attack of 9/11, Crumb by the Vietnam War. But their musical responses have been very different. Adams has produced a large public statement, using a large orchestra, performed in a concert hall; while Crumb's *Black Angels* is a personal cry of grief and despair, performed by four musicians.

Hans Werner Henze

In 1953, Hans Werner Henze left his native Germany, where he had been born in 1926, and crossed the Alps to make his home in the warm sun of Italy. He felt this departure as a great liberation.

He does not happily conform to musical fashion (or personal and political fashions, either), and this has often resulted in his music being ignored by the classical mainstream. But this very response from the academic Establishment should alert us to the possibility of an exciting, fresh voice.

Henze rebelled against the ideas of Schoenburg and Serialism. He felt, after the horrors of Nazism, that he could not follow rules in his composition. The rules of Serialism felt like a straitjacket, smothering his individuality and creativity.

The piece of music by Henze that I want to explore here is his *Symphony No. 4*, written in 1955. At this time, his music had been wonderfully touched by the warmth of the Mediterranean, and was no longer Germanic. It owes more to Debussy than Mahler, more to Respighi than Schoenberg.

The influence of nationality on classical music is a difficult subject. It is to do with a subtle interplay between a composer's individual voice and tradition. Overtly nationalist composers, like the Norwegian Grieg, or the Czech Smetana, use folk songs and rhythms, but the national flavour of a piece of music is more complex than that.

It is to do with the orchestration, and the use of modes and cadences. It is like identifying an accent, and it comes with familiarity. After a time listening to Elgar, or Vaughan Williams, you may catch yourself thinking, "This music sounds English." Or, after much Tchaikovsky and Rachmaninov, you might say "This music somehow sounds Russian." Then, when you hear some Butterworth or Borodin, you will be able to hear the English or Russian influence.

To date (2008), Henze has written ten symphonies. This fact, by itself, is worthy of note and marks him out as ploughing his own furrow.

In the nineteenth century any composer worth his salt composed symphonies. The symphony was considered the climax of the composer's art. It enabled him to make a grand public statement and make a lot of noise. He could reveal himself in an extended form that required skill and patience. It communicated the journey of a heroic soul, often through darkness to the final triumphant finale. It was primarily a spiritual and individualistic view of humanity.

However, in the twentieth century, most composers have avoided the symphony. There are major exceptions to this – Shostakovich being the most important – but in general composers have found that their experience of life does not match the heroic view. The century's new science, Psychology, has given us flawed heroes and unconscious terrors.

As a result, composers have stuck to shorter and less unified structures. A fragmented view of humanity has often led to a fragmented and discordant music.

But Henze has written symphonies, and thus is already refusing to follow the crowd. And that is a symphonic, heroic thing to do!

The Fourth Symphony is in one uninterrupted movement of nearly twenty-eight minutes. Immediately, we can recognise that this is not the conventional symphonic structure, and I am only aware of one other single movement symphony before this – Sibelius's *Seventh Symphony*.

Sibelius was trying to build a structure that reflected his view of Nature, in that it unfolded organically from a single seed. Henze seems to be doing something similar here, and in this case the seed is a long, sustained middle-C on the French Horns. It is not that the Symphony is in the key of C, but that other notes seem to gather around the C, like leaves on a tree, or layers of snow on a snowball.

From this comes the first little surge of growth, a delicate mix of instruments that sounds like the Impressionism of Debussy, and yet there are also faint echoes of film music. It makes me think of a Greek or Italian garden at night – dark, warm and heavily fragrant.

Fragments of themes come and go, like warm breezes or floating silk. Anyone can wallow in this music – just imagine somewhere you know, or know in pictures, anywhere, and imagine it on a summer night. Add beauty in whatever form you want it.

It would, however, be unfair to suggest that the *Fourth Symphony* is nothing but a warm bath. It grows very slowly, from surge to surge, so that you are always aware that something is changing, a story is being told. This is, after all, a symphony.

But the transformation of the music is slow, though inexorable. Henze is on record as saying that his favourite Italian word is *adagio*. Adagio is an Italian musical term, or instruction, meaning 'slowly, at ease'.

The early parts of the symphony seem to be dominated by light and subtle counterpoint in the woodwind, and the central sections introduce a variety of *cantabile* lines (*cantabile* means like a song line, a singing tone) by solo string instruments, which is reminiscent of the English style of Vaughan Williams.

Many critics will point to these two styles of music to point out the Italian-German mix in Henze's work. Complex counterpoint is seen as particularly German (think Bach), and cantabile is seen as typically Italian (think Italian opera). This is ludicrously simplistic, but there is a grain of truth in it.

As the symphony progresses, however, the richer sounds of the brass begin to emerge. There is still the delicate impressionistic scoring between the surges, but each surge gets grander.

At the end, the music seems to be dying away quietly into night. But this is not the end, because the final swell dispels all thoughts of darkness and night in a triumphant surge of sound that makes me think of a Mediterranean sunrise.

★ ★ ★ ★ ★

Here, then, we have four composers, living and writing at the moment, who are very different from each other, but who will repay further listening. There are many others, of course. One good way to find contemporary composers is to listen to the BBC Promenade concerts – on the radio, television or live at the Albert Hall. The Promenade concerts, which take place every August, nearly always include a new piece of music, often a world or UK premiere.

Going to Concerts – The Live Experience

Before the twentieth century all music was live, and most music was live until relatively recently. When I was under the family piano, listening to my dad, I was listening to live music, with all its imperfections, its hesitations and repetitions, and difficult bits.

It just was not part of my experience that music could come from pressing a button or turning a dial. Music needed another human being, a certain amount of skill, dexterity, and practice – hours and hours of practice! It was not something you talked over, for it had, in our house at least, a kind of ritual to it, almost a form of worship.

That might seem a bit 'over the top', but that's how it was. My father and my uncle were in semi-religious awe of the great composers, and the playing of music was, in a way, a form of contacting God. I remember my uncle saying that he expected to meet Mozart in Heaven, but that if they weren't playing his music there, my uncle didn't want to go. My dad spoke of Beethoven as some kind of manifestation of divine, pianistic energy.

With this around me it's hardly surprising that I grew up with an unquestioned respect for composers and musicians. I was an agnostic child and an atheistic adult, but I thought of live performance almost as a form of worship, with musicians as the high priests, and the audience as the congregation.

Even when I started to buy records, and then CDs, live

performances were still the real point of it all. For example, I remember going to my first live performance of William Walton's *Belshazzar's Feast* by the Halle Orchestra and Choir at the old Free Trade Hall in Manchester. I can remember every detail of the occasion, and the magnificence of the music. It is a concert that has left a memory burned into my brain, and, it seems to me, that is the mark of great art. But I don't remember the occasion when I first listened to the record I bought, nor the CD that replaced it.

There's much more where that came from: my first live experience of Mahler's *Symphony of a Thousand*, the first time I saw (why do we say we 'saw' a concert, when surely the most important thing is that we listened to it?) Bach's *Goldberg Variations*, brilliantly played by the Canadian pianist, Angela Hewitt, or the time I was swept away by Respighi's *The Pines of Rome*, or a performance of Rachmaninov's *Third Symphony* in Nottingham, played by the London Symphony Orchestra, conducted by Andre Previn.

And don't forget those concerts by *Yes*, *Pink Floyd*, and *The Grateful Dead*. The list could go on forever.

More than anything else, I suppose, live performances (concerts and recitals) are the crux of the musical experience for the listener to classical music. It is only at a concert that you get the sense of occasion that encourages total concentration on the music. That concentration is increased by the presence of lots of other concentrating people. It's almost like meditation.

That same concentration and presence of others results in a stronger emotional response, and an awareness that goes beyond the verbal and intellectual, into an area of communication that properly belongs to music alone.

Unlike a recording, the music will never sound like this again. You may not notice any difference, but the experience is unique –

you in your particular seat and in your particular body with its own particular memory and experiences – are hearing it in a different way to all the other unique bodies in the audience. Even the irritations are yours alone – the breathing of the person next to you, the uncontrollable frog in someone's throat behind you, the programme rustler in front. In this situation, the composer is communicating directly and personally with you as an individual. This cannot happen with a CD.

As you can imagine, I think going to concerts is 'a good thing'. Most times you will have a powerful experience.

Which concerts should you choose to go to? Unless you're very rich, you'll have to pick and choose. Most orchestral concerts these days consist of three items. There is no reason why this should be so, and it hasn't always been so, but it has become a habit among concert promoters.

The first piece will probably be relatively short, and will act as an entrée, an appetiser. In all likelihood it will be an Overture or a Tone Poem. The second piece will be longer, and will usually be a Concerto with a freelance soloist.

There will then be an interval. No one will think you're strange if you opt to stay in the hall and read the programme, though.

The second half of the concert will usually contain the main item – probably a Symphony. This is longer and more complex, and, if it is played well, it will receive lengthy applause, the conductor being called back to the stage many times, before the audience finally gives up and lets him go. It is not usual to shout and whistle during the applause, although isolated calls of "Bravo!" and "Encore!" are allowed if you have had a really good time.

Unlike at pop concerts, where they are seen as an essential part of the show, Encores are very rare at classical concerts, so there is no need to feel short-changed when the orchestra goes off. If an orchestra goes off the stage, they don't come back on again – imagine the logistics!

When you're trying to decide which concerts to go to, don't expect to find one in which all the music is familiar to you. You should see each concert as an opportunity for further travel, an opportunity to go somewhere new; so look at what's on, and if there is one piece of music you like in it, go to it. You'll enjoy the evening because of the piece you like, and the other two pieces may open up completely new vistas. Don't be afraid of anything – it's only music, it can't hurt you.

I have included a list of pieces I have found particularly exciting or memorable in live performance in Appendix 3. This list is personal and subjective, so just use it as a guide.

Guide to Further Exploration

If and when you decide to set off on an exploration of classical music, it will be your own journey. You will make discoveries that you would never be able to forecast, and find types of music you didn't know existed. Luckily, though, you will not be crossing a trackless void. Lots of other people have been there before you, so sometimes you can pick up a track to follow. With composers like Mozart and Beethoven it will be like a motorway, and with composers like Crumb or Macmillan it will be a case of looking for disturbed stones! But you will not feel alone.

Now for the obvious – always start from where you are. If you hear a piece of music you like – for whatever reason – listen to more music by the same composer. Then listen to other composers who write similar music.

You can find out who these composers are through this book,

or by reading the notes that come with the recording you have. If you like Beethoven, for example, you're likely to enjoy Brahms or Schubert. If you like Mozart, try Haydn.

Listen to anything and everything. If you like jazz or Broadway musicals, try Gershwin and Bernstein; if you like folk music, try Bartok or Vaughan Williams.

Use this book as a guide to new routes, some where many have been before, some less well travelled. It's really exciting, the uncertainty of a new territory, the delight of discovery and the return to the familiar. Who knows where it will lead? The possibilities for forging your own path are endless. Just follow your heart.

Appendix I
Keeping Time

43,000 BC Earliest known flute

2,000 BC Earliest known song – Assyrian

Medieval

540–604 Papacy of Pope Gregory

1098 Birth of Hildegard of Bingen, composer

1151 Hildegard composed *Ordo Virtutum,* often said to be the origin of opera

1179 Death of Hildegard of Bingen

Renaissance

1505 Birth of English composer, Thomas Tallis

1540 Birth of William Byrd

1563 Birth of John Dowland

1570 Tallis composes *Spem in Alium*

1585 Death of Thomas Tallis

1623 Death of William Byrd

1626 Death of John Dowland

Baroque

1678 Birth of Antonio Vivaldi

1685 Birth of J S Bach

1685 Handel born in Halle, Germany

1707 Bach writes *Toccata and Fugue in D Minor* for organ

1717 Premiere of Handel's *Water Music*

1721 Bach writes *The Brandenburg Concertos*

1722 Bach writes *The Well-Tempered Clavier*

1723 Vivaldi writes *The Four Seasons*

1724 Bach writes his *Mass in B Minor*

1727 Bach writes the *St. Matthew Passion*

1727 Handel becomes a British subject

1732 Birth of Haydn in Austria

1741 Bach publishes *The Goldberg Variations*

1741 Handel composes *Messiah*

1741 Death of Vivaldi in Vienna

1749 Handel composes *Music for the Royal Fireworks*

1750 Bach dies in Leipzig

1756 Birth of Mozart in Salzburg, Austria

1759 Mozart starts to play piano, age 3

1759 Death of Handel

Classical

1764 Mozart writes his first symphony, age 8

1770 Birth of Beethoven in Bonn

1788 Mozart writes his last three symphonies, No.39, 40, 41

1791 Mozart writes *The Magic Flute,* the *Requiem,* his last *Piano Concerto*

1791 Mozart dies in Vienna

1792 Beethoven moves to Vienna to study with Haydn

1800 Beethoven completes *Symphony No.1*

1801 Beethoven writes *The Moonlight Sonata*

1803 Beethoven writes is *Symphony No.3 'Eroica'*

1806 Beethoven writes his *Violin Concerto*

1808 Beethoven finishes *Symphonies No.5&6*

1809 Haydn dies in Vienna
1809 Beethoven writes *The Emperor Concerto*
1809 Mendelssohn born in Hamburg
1812 Beethoven completes Symphony No.7
1813 Birth of Wagner in Leipzig
1820 Mendelssohn's first composition, age 11
1824 Beethoven completes his *Symphony No.9 'Choral'*
1827 Death of Beethoven in Vienna
1832 Mendelssohn writes *Fingal's Cave*
1833 Brahms born in Hamburg
1833 Mendelssohn conducts premiere of *Italian Symphony*
1840 Birth of Tchaikovsky in Russia
1842 Mendelssohn completes his *Scottish Symphony*
1843 Mendelssohn writes *A Midsummer Night's Dream*
1847 Death of Mendelssohn in Leipzig

Late and Post-Romantic

1857 Birth of Elgar in Broadheath, Worcestershire
1860 Birth of Mahler in Bohemia, Austria
1862 Birth of Debussy in France
1864 Birth of Richard Strauss in Munich
1865 Birth of Sibelius in Finland
1865 Wagner composes *Tristan and Isolde*
1869 Tchaikovsky writes *Romeo and Juliet*
1870 Richard Strauss starts to compose, age 6
1873 Birth of Rachmaninov near Novgorod in Russia
1874 Birth of Schoenberg in Vienna
1875 Mahler enters Vienna Conservatoire, age 15
1875 Birth of Ravel in France
1876 Wagner completes the building of the Bayreuth Opera House
1876 Brahms first symphony completed

1876 Bayreuth opens with the premiere of Wagner's *Ring Cycle*

1880 Mahler begins working as a conductor

1882 Birth of Stravinsky in Russia

1883 Death of Wagner in Venice

1883 Birth of Webern in Vienna

1889 Mahler finishes his *Symphony No. 1*

1892 Mahler completes first version of *Symphony No. 4*

1893 Death of Tchaikovsky in St Petersburg

1897 Mahler appointed conductor of the Vienna Opera

1897 Death of Brahms in Vienna

1899 Sibelius writes *Finlandia*

1899 Elgar writes *The Enigma Variations*

1900 First performance of Elgar's *The Dream of Gerontius*

1900 Sibelius writes *Symphony No. 1*

1901 Rachmaninov writes *Piano Concerto No. 2*

1902 Mahler writes *Symphony No. 5*

1902 Sibelius writes *Symphony No. 2*

1903 Premiere of Sibelius's *Violin Concerto*

1905 Tippett born in London

1906 Birth of Shostakovich in Russia

1907 Rachmaninov writes *Symphony No. 2*

1908 Premiere of Elgar's *Symphony No. 1*

1908 Birth of Messiaen in Avignon, France

1909 Mahler finishes *Symphony No. 9*

1909 Rachmaninov writes *Piano Concerto No. 3* for his first tour of USA

1910 Premiere of Mahler's *Symphony of a Thousand*

1910 Stravinsky writes *The Firebird*

1911 Death of Mahler from heart disease

1911 Sibelius writes *Symphony No. 4*

1911 Elgar writes *Symphony No. 2*

Modern

1913 Premiere of Stravinsky's *Rite of Spring*
1917 Rachmaninov emigrates to Denmark, then USA
1918 Death of Debussy
1919 Elgar writes his *Cello Concerto*
1919 Sibelius writes *Symphony No. 5*
1924 Sibelius writes *Symphony No. 7*
1925 Shostakovich writes *Symphony No. 1*, age 19
1926 Sibelius writes *Tapiola*
1926 Birth of Hans Werner Henze in Germany
1928 Stockhausen born near Cologne
1929 Birth of George Crumb in West Virginia
1930 Birth of Takemitsu in Japan
1933 Birth of Gorecki in Poland
1934 Death of Elgar
1935 Birth of Arvo Part in Estonia
1937 Death of Ravel

Neo-Classical

1939 Tippett writes *Concerto for Double String Orchestra*
1941 Tippett composes *A Child of Our Time*
1941 Stockhausen's mother killed by euthanasia by Nazis
1943 Death of Rachmaninov
1944 Birth of Tavener in London
1945 Tippett composes his *Symphony No. 1*
1945 Death of Webern in Austria
1947 Birth of John Adams in Worcester, Massachusetts
1948 Messiaen composes *The Turangalila Symphony*
1949 Death of Richard Strauss
1950 Stockhausen starts to compose
1951 Death of Schoenberg in Los Angeles
1952 Stockhausen starts studying under Messiaen

1953 Tippett writes *Fantasia Concertante on a Theme by Corelli*
1955 Stockhausen develops concept of *group-composition*
1955 Henze writes *Symphony No. 4*

Post-Modern

1956 Stockhausen writes *Gesang der Junglinge*
1957 Stockhausen writes *Gruppen*
1957 Death of Sibelius in Finland
1959 Birth of James Macmillan in Ayrshire, Scotland
1961 Birth of Michael Torke in Milwaukee, USA
1964 Messiaen writes *Et Expecto Resurrectionem*
1964 Part writes *Collage on B-A-C-H*
1968 Stockhausen composes *Stimmung*
1970 George Crumb writes *Black Angels*
1971 Death of Stravinsky in New York
1975 Death of Shostakovich in Russia
1977 Part writes *Tabula Rasa*
1978 Part writes *Spiegel im Spiegel*
1987 Adams writes *The Chairman Dances*
1992 Death of Messiaen in Paris
1993 Tavener writes *Song for Athene*
1995 Tippett composes *The Rose Lake*
1996 Death of Takemitsu
1998 Tippett dies in London of pneumonia
2002 Adams writes *On the Transmigration of Souls*
2007 Death of Stockhausen

Appendix 2
Keys

If you are a musician, you almost grow up with the concept of keys, but if you don't play an instrument, as I didn't when I was young, they can be totally perplexing. If we allow it to, the language of keys can make the whole of classical music seem impenetrable and irrelevant.

For many years I just ignored it, and I still wouldn't be able to tell you what key a piece of music was in just by listening to it. But, as I will explain, you don't need to know everything to be able to hear most of what is happening

The idea of a key is based on the *scale*. In Western music, the octave is divided into twelve equal notes, as I mentioned when I was talking about equal temperament, but the scale is a group of seven of those notes that seem to us to sound right as a group.

This is demonstrated by what is known as the *tonic sol fa*, which is doh, ray, mi, fa, soh, lah, te, doh. A scale, then, is the notes as sung in the song from the musical, *The Sound of Music*. You can start with doh on any pitch you choose, and this is called a *movable tonic sol fa*.

A scale is a climbing or falling ladder of notes that we in the West feel sound right. The scale of C begins and ends on C; the scale of G sharp begins and ends on G sharp, and so on.

Each note has two scales – a major and minor. People generally feel that major scales sound confident and happy, whereas minor scales sound sad and introspective. So C major begins and ends on C, and will sound extrovert; C minor will also begin and end on C, but will sound sad.

Musicians will be throwing their hands in the air at this point at how simplistic I am being, but this explanation will do for me.

A piece of music in the key of C major will only use the notes that are in the scale of C major. If the composer puts in a note that isn't in the scale, it will sound wrong. The tune can start on any note the composer wishes, but, if he or she only uses the notes of the C major scale, the tune will only sound finished on C. Finish the tune on any note other than C and it will feel unfinished, or unresolved.

Because of this the note C is the most important one in the key of C and is called the *tonic*. Natural overtones, or harmonies, make G the next most important, and this is called the *dominant*. F is also important, and is called the *sub-dominant*, because it is one note below the dominant. So you can see that keys are hierarchical, and all notes are equal but some notes are more equal than others!

All keys, therefore, have a tonic, which is the keynote; a dominant, which is five notes above the tonic; and a sub-dominant, which is four notes above the tonic. The other notes of a scale, or key, also have names, although these notes are not so important and you don't really need to know them. Just for the sake of tidiness, however, here are all the names of the seven notes of the scale: tonic, supertonic, median, sub-dominant, dominant, sub-median, and leading-note.

To further complicate matters, some people believe that certain keys have particular feelings associated with them. This is somewhat controversial.

The idea of the moveable tonic sol fa suggests that it really doesn't matter what note you start on, so long as all the other notes maintain the same relationship with each other. In other words, if you sing a song in the key of C or in the key of A it will be the same. It will just be higher or lower, that's all.

However, certain keys have been favoured by composers for

particular types of music, and this has given rise to the belief that a tune in G, for example, has a different 'emotional charge' to a tune in F. It is a chicken and egg question.

Those who support the idea of keys having an extrinsic meaning say, for example, that the key of F has a rural, countryside feel to it, and point out the fact that Beethoven's *Pastoral Symphony* is in F. Similarly, the key of E flat is supposed to be noble and expansive, and Elgar's *Nimrod* from *The Enigma Variations* is in E flat. These are just examples – there are many examples of these clusters of types of music in specific keys, and you can make your own mind up as you wish, because no two people seem to agree about it!

Appendix 3
Live Magic

Here is a list of pieces of music I have found particularly exciting or memorable in live performances. It is in no way prescriptive – it is just a personal guide. Feel free to ignore it.

Adams (1947–)
The Chairman Dances (1987)
John Adams is an American Minimalist composer who has found himself enmeshed in the world of Opera. By its nature, opera tells a story, which is not something Minimalists are supposed to do. This has required Adams to invent *Post-Minimalism*, because if he writes Post-Minimalist music, the critics will allow him to write operas! *The Chairman Dances* is an orchestral concert piece linked to his successful opera, *Nixon in China*. I first heard this in Manchester, conducted by the composer, and I was thrilled by its immediacy and foot-tapping accessibility. I recommend you listen to any Adams you can find.

Barber (1910–1981)
Adagio for Strings (1936)
Barber's *Adagio for Strings* is really well known, now that popular radio has discovered it. It has a special memory for me, because it was the last piece of music my father listened to when he was

dying – the radio tells us it's relaxing (it seems that everything is sold to us on this basis – is this the only state music can instil?), but I find it unbearably sad and yearning. Don't be frightened of feeling things – shake off that stupor of relaxation!

Bax (1883–1953)
Tintagel (1919)
Arnold Bax is not a particularly well-known English composer. I first listened to this because of the title, which refers to the putative King Arthur ruins on the wild and craggy cliffs of Tintagel in Cornwall.

Beethoven (1770–1827)
Symphony No.5 (1808)
If you don't know it, any Beethoven piece is worth going to hear. However, I would tend to avoid concerts with more than one piece by him. Why? I suppose I want to find new composers and new music. Beethoven's *Fifth Symphony* is probably the most widely recognised piece of classical music ever written. It suffers from this popularity, however, because we have stopped listening carefully to it, and because we tend to forget there is much more to it than those first four notes. Exciting stuff, and good if you want a dose of heroic optimism.

Berlioz (1803–1869)
Symphonie Fantastique (1830)
This symphony is stereotypical Romantic music. I first heard it on record – it was on a 12-inch record that was given away with the first issue of a magazine called *The Great Musicians*. This magazine – it was a little booklet, really, containing the composer's life story and a detailed analysis of the music on the record plus the free record – cost about 13 shillings! I still think

the recording was better than any I have heard since! This symphony tells a story in music, but you won't know what it is from the music alone, which I think is ultimately a serious problem with a lot of what is called *Programme Music* – that is, music for which you need a programme to explain it. The story here is of Berlioz's unrequited love for an English actress and related opium-induced dreams and nightmares. It's a good romp, but if you go to a concert of it, buy and read the programme!

Bernstein (1918–1990)
Symphonic Dances from West Side Story (1957)

I'm not a big fan of the Broadway musical, but if I had to choose the one I consider to be the best of the genre, I would cite *West Side Story*. With a basic story by Shakespeare, a book by Stephen Sondheim, and music by Leonard Bernstein, how could it not be the greatest musical? At a live performance of this, one of the things you notice about the orchestra, before they play a note, is the size of the percussion section. This is always a sign of high-energy music – in fact, I went through a period when I could accurately forecast my enjoyment of a concert by the number of percussionists!

Brahms (1833–1897)
Symphony No. 1 (1876); *Violin Concerto* (1878)

You will have no trouble finding a Brahms concert – they're everywhere. I find his music a bit turgid, a bit unremarkable, but when I first heard his *First Symphony* as a teenager, I thought, "Here is wisdom, here is the measured tread of maturity." And he has such damn good tunes, and rich harmonies!

Britten (1913–1979)
Four Sea Interludes from Peter Grimes (1945)

Benjamin Britten was the largest figure in English music in the second half of the twentieth century. He is mainly known for his Operas, of which *Peter Grimes* is one, but he also wrote a stupendous *War Requiem*, commissioned for the opening of the new Coventry Cathedral, and many other accessible pieces. *The Four Sea Interludes* were taken by Britten from his opera, *Peter Grimes*, and put together for the concert hall. They are a magnificent evocation of the cold bleakness of the East Coast, where he lived.

Bruckner (1824–1896)
Symphony No.4 Romantic (1874)

Many people can't stand Bruckner. He can be laborious, slow to build his musical ideas, ponderous in his orchestration, and his symphonies are too long; but his Fourth Symphony, in my opinion, is his best and his least rambling. If you like Romantic music, and you like your music laid on with a trowel, Bruckner is the man for you. The only adjective you need for Bruckner is 'big'. Sometimes I love him.

Copland (1900–1990)
Appalachian Spring (1944)

Many people consider Aaron Copland to be America's greatest composer. You, of course, don't have to agree. Judgements like that are a bit silly really. I only mention it so you know what others might think if they want to engage you in a conversation about American classical music. This is not, luckily, very likely – it has never happened to me. Bernstein and Copland were friends, and Bernstein was a big exponent of Copland's music, so if you get a recording of a Copland piece, get one conducted by Bernstein, as they are still pretty definitive.

Dvorak (1841–1904)
Symphony No.9 From the New World (1893)
Dvorak was a Czech Nationalist composer. His *New World Symphony* is extremely popular. The theme from the slow movement seems to have been indelibly tattooed into the British consciousness as something to do with a certain brand of brown bread, but actually, the theme is Dvorak's take on Black American Spirituals (so successful that it has since become one, with words written to fit it), and it has absolutely nothing to do with nostalgia, England, a Yorkshire accent, or anything like that. Try to forget it if you can.

Elgar (1857–1934)
The Enigma Variations (1899); *Symphony No.1* (1908); *Cello Concerto* (1919)
This is quintessential English music, coming out of Edwardian England, when it was always summer and when God was an Englishman. It is full of good tunes and stirring harmonies, though his later work tends to be more uncertain. Elgar wrote *Land of Hope and Glory*, which is a good tune as well – he is not responsible for the words.

Gershwin (1898–1937)
Rhapsody in Blue (1924); *Piano Concerto* (1925)
Gershwin's music is thoroughly American. Jazz and Broadway heavily influence both of these works. His piano parts are exciting and fun, and he puts you in a good mood.

Hanson (1896–1981)
Symphony No.2 Romantic (1939)
An American Post-Romantic, Hanson has been somewhat overlooked. I first heard this symphony in the car – it was one of

those times when I just had to sit there after I had reached my destination to listen to the end and find out what it was called.

Janacek (1854–1928)
Taras Bulba (1918); *Sinfonietta* (1926)
Janacek (pronounced y*anna-check*) was a Hungarian Nationalist, and his orchestral music is wild and evokes the endless flat steppes of Eastern Europe.

Macmillan born (1959 –)
The Confession of Isobel Gowdie (1990)
James Macmillan is a Scottish composer who is beginning to get noticed. His music is Post-Modernist and quite savage at times. His work, *The Confession of Isobel Gowdie*, received a rapturous response at its premiere at the Proms. It is MacMillan's response to the persecution of witches in seventeenth century Scotland. Isobel Gowdie was one of these women – in her case she was from Nairn – and MacMillan describes this as an apology for all the suffering caused by the witch persecutions, and as the Requiem Isobel never had. As you can imagine, the music is frightening and the orchestration is a good example of how Post-Modernist composers use traditional instruments in new ways.

Mahler (1860–1911)
Symphony No.2 The Resurrection (1894);
Symphony No.4 (1900); *Symphony No.8 Symphony of a Thousand* (1906)
Mahler, like Bruckner and Wagner, is big, really big. These symphonies are the last heroic cries of Romanticism, but also the first cries of twentieth century dissonance. Mahler uses huge orchestras (he must have been able to get his hands on lots of fairly cheap musicians – maybe aided by his international reputation as

a conductor). The Second and the Eighth also involve a choir – just in terms of volume alone, Mahler's symphonies are overwhelming. If you like your music clean and sparse you may well find this music ridiculously 'over the top', but just abandon yourself to it and you will be washed up on the shore at the end, exhausted and feeling emotionally drained. It is therapeutic to go through this from time to time, or if you have had too much Stravinsky, or Webern, or even Mozart. Mahler reminds us that music is all about an emotional response to an emotional stimulus.

Maxwell Davies (1934 –)
An Orkney Wedding with Sunrise (1984)
Peter Maxwell Davies is a Manchester composer who lives in the remote Orkney Islands, off the north coast of Scotland. This particular piece of music is great fun, as the musicians at an Orkney wedding get more and more drunk as the party goes through the night. When all has dissolved into a drunken musical mess, the sunrise arrives in the form of a solo bagpiper. In a live performance, this moment is magical, as the piper enters from the back of the hall (at least, he did when I saw it), and marches to the front, to join the orchestra.

Mendelssohn (1809–1847)
The Hebrides Overture Fingal's Cave (1830);
Symphony No.4 Italian (1833); *Violin Concerto* (1844)
In my opinion, Mendelssohn is much abused. Musical snobs talk about him, if they condescend to do so at all, as lightweight, derivative, too easy. Like Mozart, he died in his thirties, and his music is exquisite, almost Classical in its grace and balance. He lacks the raw emotional power of Beethoven and he is certainly no revolutionary figure, but then, nor was Mozart. This music is easy to listen to, and that is no criticism.

Mozart (1756–1791)
Symphony No.41 Jupiter (1788)

It seems wrong to only mention one work by Mozart, but that is because he was extraordinarily prolific and all of his music is worth listening to. He is generally considered to be classical music's greatest genius – a child prodigy of prodigious proportions! His music is regularly performed and recorded and played on radio and television. You can even hear loads of it on telephone-recorded messages, in lifts and shopping malls, on mobile phone ring tones, and in tv adverts. You will know lots of Mozart already! Go to hear his music at concerts, but be selective, or you will have no money left to hear anyone else. Too much Mozart is like too many chocolate éclairs.

Rachmaninov (1873–1943)
Symphony No.2 (1907); *Piano Concerto No.3* (1909)

Rachmaninov seems to be going through a huge increase in popularity at the moment. There are fashions in composers as in everything else. The slow movement from his *Second Piano Concerto* was made famous by its use in the film *Brief Encounter*. In his day he was better known as a great pianist, and his works for piano are incredibly difficult. My dad hero-worshipped him, but as a pianist, not as a composer. His symphonies are lush, and prefigure much romantic film music, and his *Third Piano Concerto* is one of the great summits of a pianist's career.

Ravel (1875–1937)
Bolero (1928)

Maurice Ravel was a French Impressionist composer. His *Piano Concerto* is well worth listening to, but I have cited *Bolero* because it is a magnificent live experience, as it very slowly adds instrument after instrument till we reach an orchestral climax that is shattering. Try to forget images of ice skaters, and listen to the orchestration!

Reich (1936 –)
Different Trains (1988)

Steve Reich is one of the most important American Minimalists. He didn't train as a musician, and studied Philosophy at University. He learned to play African drums, and, after meeting John Cage, decided to compose. I have heard (on television) his piece, *Different Trains*, described as the greatest music of the twentieth century. I have heard the same said about Stravinsky's *Rite of Spring*, and of Cage's *4:33*. As far as I'm concerned, Stravinsky wins hands down! However, *Different Trains* is a powerful piece about the role of the railways in the events of the Holocaust and the Jewish migration across America. It is performed by a combination of a string quartet and taped sections of train noises and the edited speech patterns of American voices. It is hypnotic, and achieves its emotional impact through its musical clarity.

Respighi (1879–1936)
The Pines of Rome (1924)

Respighi was an Italian Impressionist. The climax of *The Pines of Rome* is very powerful in concert, and I remember hearing it in the Yorkshire town of Halifax – I had never heard of Respighi before, which made the experience even more powerful. Never be put off a concert because it contains music by someone you've never heard of – it might open a door to a whole new world for you to explore.

Rutter (1945 –)
Requiem (1985)

John Rutter was in the same school choir as John Tavener. He is a very popular and accessible writer of religious music for choirs, and if you sing in a choir you will almost certainly have sung something by him. The *Requiem* is for choir and orchestra, and is very easy to listen to. If you have problems with listening to choral music, Rutter could well be the place to start.

Saint Saens (1835–1921)
Symphony No.3 Organ Symphony (1886)

I remember sitting in the car with my uncle, listening to the *Organ Symphony* on the radio, having gone to buy a takeaway curry. We both knew the music, and could sing along with it, but we couldn't identify it. I remember Mahler was one of our guesses. The curry was going cold as we sat outside the house, determined to crack the puzzle we had set ourselves. The organ doesn't enter until the last movement, and when it did we both jumped out of the car shouting, "The *Organ Symphony!*" People must have thought we were mad. So did the others in the house when we opened the takeaway to reveal the cold, coagulating oil on top of the curry!

Schubert (1797–1828)
Symphony No.9 The Great C major (1825)

Schubert was another composer who died young. The Romantics, of course, loved that sort of thing – oh, the tragedy! The pain! Schubert's reputation stems largely from the songs he wrote, but he also wrote some fine symphonies. His Ninth Symphony was one of the first records my dad bought, an RCA recording, conducted by Toscanini. The first version you get to know of a piece of music is nearly always your favourite, but when that version is a Toscanini interpretation, the search for a better version is doomed to failure.

Shostakovich (1906–1975)
Symphony No.5 (1937)

Shostakovich is the great symphonist of the twentieth century. The symphony was not a popular form in the twentieth century, but Shostakovich seemed to revel in the grand, public gesture of the form, although, if you want a little more honesty and intimacy, you should go to his Chamber Music. The *Fifth Symphony* was written to escape fatal criticism by Stalin, and, on one level, this music can be heard as the triumphant struggle of State Communism against the forces of Formalism. However, much has been written about Shostakovich's hidden codes and musical quotations, so that now the music seems to be a clever and disguised criticism of Stalin. The audience wept at its first performance, and the slow movement sounds like a long cry of pain for lost innocence.

Sibelius (1865–1947)
Symphony No.2 (1901)

As you know, Sibelius was my personal favourite, so you can hardly expect a balanced entry here. Obviously, I think you should listen to everything he composed. As a starter, though, you might like to try a live performance of his *Second Symphony*. The Finale is magical, building climax on climax till the big tune seems to finally take off and fly. His fourth and seventh symphonies are also worthy of special mention, as are all the others!

Stravinsky (1882–1971)
The Rite of Spring 1913

In my opinion, the seminal work of the twentieth century. This is dynamic, forceful, and full of energy. It is dominated by rhythm and dissonance, and is an absolute must for anyone wishing to paddle in the Modern Sea. Stravinsky was nothing if not versatile, and his work includes Post-Romantic, Neo-Classical, and Serialist music.

Takemitsu (1930–1996)
From me flows what you call Time (1990)

Takemitsu is the modern Debussy. He learned his music while listening to swing bands on American bases, and developed a form of music in which he combined the Impressionism of Debussy with the Gamelan music of Indonesia, and the philosophy of Japan, after meeting John Cage. I find his music fascinating – delicate and shimmering, with a percussive strength. And it satisfies my desire for lots of percussion!

Tallis (c1505–1585)
Spem in Alium (c1570)

Spem in Alium has to be the flower of the English Renaissance. It is a fourty part motet, which means that it combines forty different lines of music into a complex choral counterpoint. The result has power and serenity at the same time.

Tavener born (1944 –)
Song for Athene (1993)

John Tavener is a choral composer, who, because he has converted to the Greek Orthodox Church, uses middle-eastern modes and harmonies. His music first came to my attention when it was used at the funeral of Diana, Princess of Wales.

Tchaikovsky (1840–1893)
Romeo and Juliet (1871); Symphony No.6 Pathetique (1893)

Tchaikovsky's life was sensationally depicted in Ken Russell's film, *The Music Lovers*. Although the film is not noted for its faithful attention to accuracy, it got me, at least, interested in the music. I don't think it matters what door to the music you open, so long as you go in and look round. The *Pathetique* was one of my dad's records, on the Marble Arch label, and I found it unbearably sad. When you listen to Tchaikovsky, expect the emotional content of the music to go over the top. When he is happy, he's very very happy, when he's in love he's completely besotted, and when he's down, he's suicidal. It's what makes him such good listening when you're young.

Tippett (1905–1997)
Concerto for Double String Orchestra (1938)

This is what has been called 'English cow-pat music' by people who don't like it – probably because it's nice to listen to! Compositions for string orchestra sound very English, and, in this work, Tippett exploits the sound to its fullest, using the Baroque grouping of two orchestras and a small group of soloists to produce wonderful music. Tippett can be quite difficult, but this piece is not. Rhythmically complex outer movements flank the beautiful slow movement.

Vaughan Williams (1872–1958)
Fantasia on a Theme by Thomas Tallis (1910); Symphony No.7 Sinfonia Antarctica (1952)

Vaughan Williams is one of the great English composers of the twentieth century. He was an avid collector of folk songs, recording them onto wax cylinders. In photographs he often appears as a venerable old man, but he wasn't always old, and saw action in the First World War, which resulted in his unofficial requiem for the dead and the old way of life in his *Third Symphony*. The *Sinfonia Antarctica* was written as the soundtrack for the film, *Scott of the Antarctic*.

Vivaldi (1678–1741)
The Four Seasons (1725)

The Four Seasons is the piece of music most likely to drive you mad, because it is the one you're most likely to hear on the phone when you're put on hold or put at the back of a queue. This is unfortunate, because these four concertos are little gems. Vivaldi wrote loads of concertos – probably hundreds – but these are the best known.

Wagner (1813–1883)
Overture to Tristan and Isolde (1865)

It was a long time before I got into Wagner. His music was a favourite of the Nazis and was played to the victims as they entered the gas chambers of Auschwitz, and it took me a long time to forgive him for that – although he was long dead by then. The music was particularly enjoyed by Hitler because Wagner was anti-Semitic. However, the music is rich and luscious, pure passion and ecstasy, and the beginning of *Tristan and Isolde* contains what has been dubbed 'The Tristan Chord', which is the first unresolved dissonance in classical music.

Walton (1902–1983)
Belshazzar's Feast (1931)

William Walton was born in Oldham. *Belshazzar's Feast* is a tremendous example of that peculiarly English musical form, the Oratorio. Other examples are Handel's *Messiah*, and *The Dream of Gerontius* by Elgar. Walton's work is exciting and dramatic, and I go and hear it whenever I can, as I always leave with a big grin on my face.

So where does all this leave us? I'll be honest — I hope it leaves you in a position where you might decide to give a classical concert a try. Go to a concert with a friend or on your own — they are rarely sold out. Remember the Chinese proverb that the journey of a thousand miles begins with a single footstep.